BOOK-1

MATHEMATICAL REASONING

THROUGH VERBAL ANALYSIS

written by

WARREN HILL & RONALD EDWARDS

© 1988

MIDWEST PUBLICATIONS

P.O. BOX 448
PACIFIC GROVE, CA 93950
ISBN 0-89455-347-X

ACKNOWLEDGEMENT

The authors and the publisher are grateful to David Lance Goines and his publisher, David R. Godine, Publisher, Inc., of Boston, for permission to use Mr. Goines' design on the cover of this book.

— A VERY IMPORTANT COMMENT —

MATHEMATICAL REASONING THROUGH VERBAL ANALYSIS is a book of math activities designed to be used in a cooperative learning situation. The activities are deceptively simple in appearance. It is essential that the teacher read the Teacher's Manual before beginning the lesson. Only in this way can he/she become fully aware of the multilayered learning that takes place when students explore all the information that can be gleaned from one exercise.

The materials were **not** designed to be used as an independent workbook. After the teacher has thoroughly <u>discussed</u> the example, and introduced and defined any vocabulary that is new to the students, the class may proceed to work the next few exercises independently or in a small group. However, the students will not receive full value from the lesson unless each exercise is <u>discussed</u> in the manner outlined in the Teacher's Manual.

As a result of exploring each exercise to the fullest extent, layer by layer, the students should show significant gains in vocabulary development, increase observation skills substantially, and be able to process mathematical concepts on a much higher level.

TABLE OF CONTENTS

MEASUREMENT

RELATIONS

TABLES AND GRAPHS

HOW MANY DOTS?

Draw lines to match the pictures of dots with the numbers.

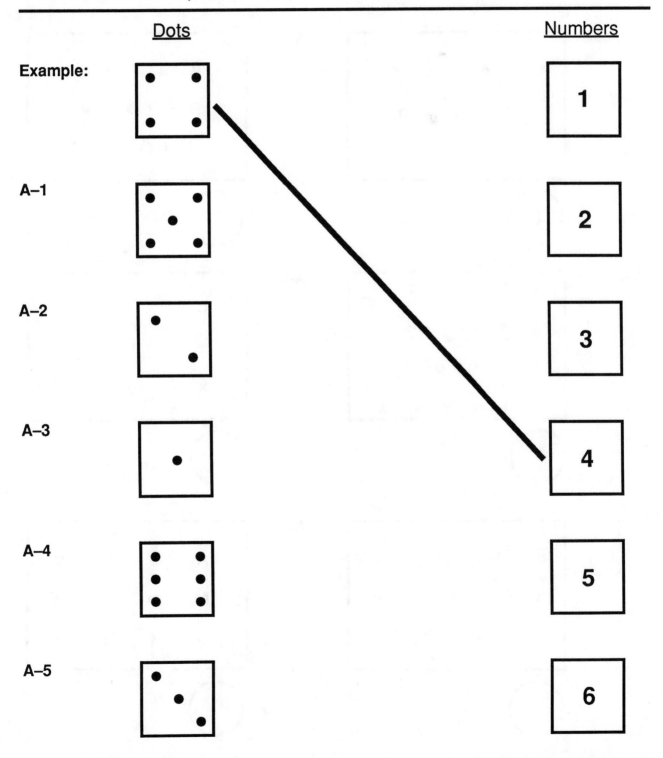

HOW MANY LETTERS?

Find the number of letters in each box.
Write the answer in the circle.

Example:

a   c

e   t   p

f

(6)

A–6

A M P F

R S T X L V

B O P M Q

( )

A–7

a b c d e f

g h i j k l

m n o p q r

s t u v w x

( )

A–8

o   r

t

x   y   z

( )

A–9

c   v   g   j   i

h   f   e

d   w   h   b

( )

A–10

A   b   C   d

M   n   O   p

S   t   U   v

( )

HOW MANY DOTS?

Each box contains pictures of four sets of dots.
Count the total number of dots in the box.
Write the answer in the circle.

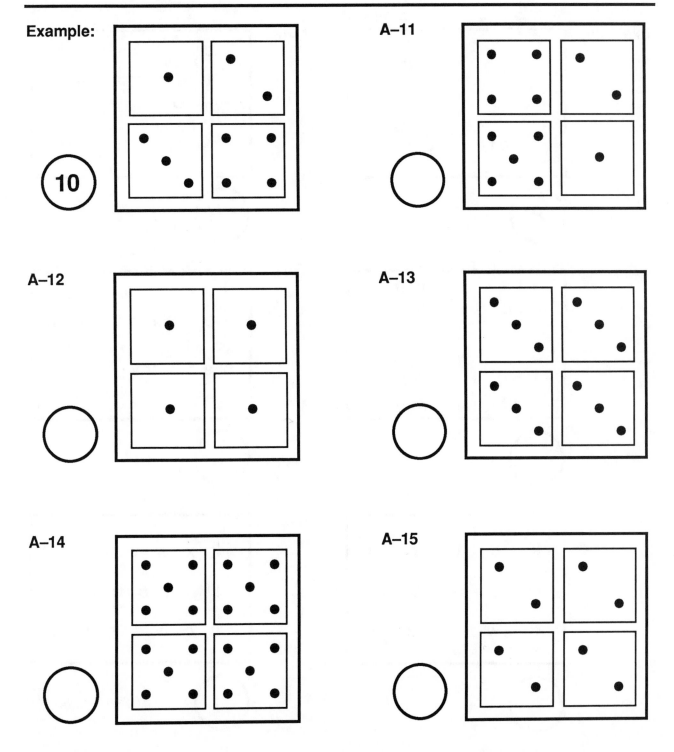

HOW MANY LETTERS?

Find the number of letters in each box.
Write the answer in the circle.

Example:

a b   c d
e f   g h

(8)

A–16

c   n
i   o   v
o
r
y
l

( )

A–17

r s   m n
t u   o p
c d   k l
e f   m n

( )

A–18

a b   r s   m n
c   t   o
d e   u v   p q

( )

A–19

k d o p q
r j s t u
v w n k l

( )

A–20

k x w v u t s
l y d c b a x
p c h e t s r

( )

4   P.O. BOX 448, PACIFIC GROVE, CA 93950

HOW MANY LETTERS?

Find the number of letters in each box. Count the <u>letters</u> only.
Write the answer in the circle.

Example:

a	2	b	3
c	5	d	e
8	4	m	9

(**6**)

A–21

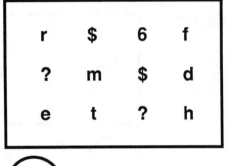

r	$	6	f
?	m	$	d
e	t	?	h

( )

A–22

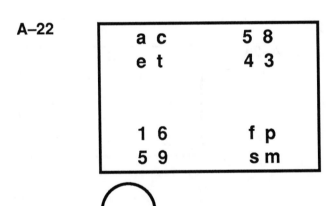

a c		5 8
e t		4 3
1 6		f p
5 9		s m

( )

A–23

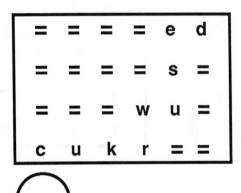

=	=	=	=	e	d
=	=	=	=	s	=
=	=	=	w	u	=
c	u	k	r	=	=

( )

A–24

=	m	p	s	i
o	f	=	e	t
c	v	h	r	=

( )

A–25

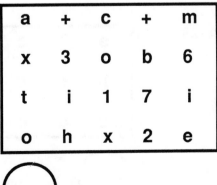

a	+	c	+	m
x	3	o	b	6
t	i	1	7	i
o	h	x	2	e

( )

HOW MANY DIFFERENT LETTERS?

Look at the boxes below. Each box contains a mixture of letters.
Find the number of different letters in each box.
Write the answer in the circle.

Example:

a	b	c
a	c	b
c	a	b

③

A–26

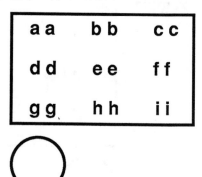

a a	b b	c c
d d	e e	f f
g g	h h	i i

◯

A–27

t	v	t	u
t	u	t	v
t	v	t	u

◯

A–28

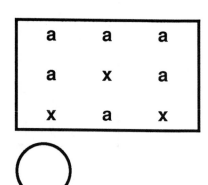

a	a	a
a	x	a
x	a	x

◯

A–29

a	b	c	d
b	c	d	e
c	d	e	f

◯

A–30

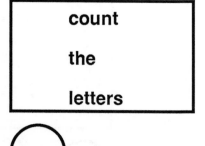

count
the
letters

◯

6   P.O. BOX 448, PACIFIC GROVE, CA 93950

HOW MANY LETTERS IN A LIST?

Each list below is part of the alphabet. The lists have missing letters.
Put the missing letters in the boxes.
Count the number of letters in each list and write the answer in the circle.

Example: a   b | c | d   e   f   (6)

A–31   e   f   g   ☐   i   j   k   l   m   ◯

A–32   s   ☐   u   v   ◯

A–33   g   h   i   ☐   k   ◯

A–34   p   q   ☐   ☐   ☐   u   v   ◯

A–35   k   l   m   ☐   ☐   ☐   ☐   ☐   s   ◯

A–36   r   s   t   u   ☐   ☐   ☐   ◯

A–37   ☐   ☐   c   d   e   ◯

HOW MANY LETTERS IN A LIST?

Each list below is part of the alphabet. The lists have missing letters.
Put the missing letters in the boxes.
Count the number of letters in each list and write the answer in the circle.

A–38   s   ☐ ☐ ☐   w   ◯

A–39   d   ☐ ☐ ☐ ☐ ☐   j   k   ◯

A–40   b   ☐ ☐ ☐ ☐   g   ◯

A–41   ☐ ☐ ☐ ☐   x   y   z   ◯

A–42   ☐ ☐ ☐ ☐   h   ☐   ◯

A–43   ☐ ☐ ☐ ☐   p   ◯

A–44   ☐ ☐ ☐ ☐   t   ◯

A–45   ☐ ☐ ☐ ☐ ☐   k   ☐   ◯

          P.O. BOX 448, PACIFIC GROVE, CA 93950

HOW MANY LETTERS IN A LIST?

Three dots means a list continues.

a b c • • • j	means	a b c d e f g h i j

This list has 10 letters.
Write the missing letters in each list in the boxes.
Write the number of letters in the list in the circle.

Example: a   b   c   •   •   •   f

a   b   c   [d]   [e]   f   (6)

A–46   c   d   e   •   •   •   j

c   d   e   [ ]   [ ]   [ ]   [ ]   j   ( )

A–47   p   q   r   •   •   •   v

p   q   r   [ ]   [ ]   [ ]   v   ( )

A–48   m   n   •   •   •   t

m   n   [ ]   [ ]   [ ]   [ ]   [ ]   t   ( )

A–49   k   l   •   •   •   s

k   l   [ ]   [ ]   [ ]   [ ]   [ ]   [ ]   s   ( )

HOW MANY LETTERS IN A LIST?

Three dots means a list continues.
Find the number of letters in each list below.
Write the answer in the circle.

Example: r   s   t   •   •   •   z   ⑨

A–50   p   q   •   •   •   t   ◯

A–51   e   f   •   •   •   n   ◯

A–52   f   •   •   •   o   ◯

A–53   a   b   c   •   •   •   z   ◯

A–54   a   b   c   •   •   •   x   ◯

A–55   c   d   e   •   •   •   z   ◯

A–56   c   •   •   •   x   ◯

HOW MANY NUMBERS IN A LIST?

The lists below have missing numbers.
Put the missing numbers in the boxes.
Count the numbers in each list and write the answer in the circle.

Example:	3	4	5	**6**	**7**	8	**⑥**
A–57	1	2	☐	☐	5		◯
A–58	7	8	☐	☐	☐	12	◯
A–59	8	9	☐	☐			◯
A–60	10	11	12	☐	☐	☐	◯
A–61	22	23	24	☐	☐		◯
A–62	35	36	☐	☐	39		◯
A–63	50	☐	☐	☐	☐	55	◯

P.O. BOX 448, PACIFIC GROVE, CA 93950

HOW MANY NUMBERS IN A LIST?

The lists below have missing numbers.
Put the missing numbers in the boxes.
Count the numbers in each list and write the answer in the circle.

A–64   5   6   ☐ ☐   9   ◯

A–65   11   ☐ ☐ ☐   15   16   ◯

A–66   20   ☐ ☐ ☐ ☐   25   ◯

A–67   31   ☐ ☐   34   ☐ ☐ ☐   ◯

A–68   ☐ ☐ ☐   17   18   19   ◯

A–69   ☐ ☐ ☐   30   31   32   ◯

A–70   ☐ ☐   19   ☐ ☐   ◯

A–71   13   12   11   ☐ ☐   8   ◯

HOW MANY NUMBERS IN A LIST?

Three dots means a list continues.

2 3 4 • • • 9 10   means   2 3 4 5 6 7 8 9 10

This list has 9 numbers.

Write the missing numbers in the boxes.

Count the numbers in each list and write the answer in the circle.

Example: 1   2   3   •   •   •   6   ⑥

1   2   3   **4**   **5**   6

A–72   3   4   5   •   •   •   9   ◯

3   4   5   ☐ ☐ ☐   9

A–73   11   12   13   •   •   •   18   ◯

11   12   13   ☐ ☐ ☐ ☐   18

A–74   30   31   •   •   •   38   ◯

30   31   ☐ ☐ ☐ ☐ ☐ ☐   38

A–75   50   51   •   •   •   58   ◯

50   51   ☐ ☐ ☐ ☐ ☐ ☐   58

HOW MANY NUMBERS IN A LIST?

Three dots means a list continues.
The circle shows how many numbers are in each list.
Find the last number in each list and write it in the box.

							Last Number	Number in List
Example:	4	5	6	•	•	•	**9**	6
A–76	1	2	3	•	•	•		6
A–77	10	11	12	•	•	•		8
A–78	21	22	23	•	•	•		5
A–79	9	10	11	•	•	•		7
A–80	1	2	3	•	•	•		9
A–81	1	2	3	•	•	•		20

P.O. BOX 448, PACIFIC GROVE, CA 93950

SEQUENCES OF NUMBERS

Place numbers in the blank spaces to continue the sequence.

Example: 9 10 11 12 **13**   **14**   **15**   **16**

A–82   17   18   19   ____   ____   ____

A–83   15   16   17   18   ____   ____   ____   ____

A–84   51   52   53   ____   ____   ____

A–85   90   91   92   ____   ____   ____   ____

A–86   64   65   66   ____   ____   ____

A–87   7   8   ____   ____   ____   ____

A–88   30   31   ____   ____   ____   ____

SEQUENCES OF NUMBERS

Place numbers in the blank spaces to continue the sequence.

A–89	14	13	12	11	____	____	____
A–90	20	19	18	____	____	____	
A–91	93	92	91	____	____	____	____
A–92	32	33	34	____	____	____	
A–93	42	41	40	____	____	____	____
A–94	9	8	____	____	____		
A–95	59	58	____	____	____	____	
A–96	62	61	____	____	____		

P.O. BOX 448, PACIFIC GROVE, CA 93950

COMPLETING THE SEQUENCE

Place numbers in the blank spaces to complete the sequence.

Example: 1   __2__   __3__   __4__   5   __6__   7

A–97   4   ____   6   ____   8   ____   10

A–98   ____   84   85   ____   ____   88

A–99   ____   19   ____   ____   22   23   24

A–100   55   ____   ____   58   59   ____   ____

A–101   ____   ____   13   14   15   ____

A–102   ____   30   ____   ____   33   ____   35

A–103   ____   ____   17   ____   ____   20

COMPLETING THE SEQUENCE

Place numbers in the blank spaces to complete the sequence.

A–104   _____   _____   93   92   91   _____   _____

A–105   _____   84   85   _____   _____   88   _____

A–106   24   23   22   _____   _____   19

A–107   17   _____   15   _____   13   _____   11

A–108   9   _____   _____   _____   5   4   _____

A–109   10   _____   8   _____   6   _____   _____

A–110   _____   _____   47   48   _____   _____   _____

A–111   72   _____   _____   _____   68   _____   _____

CONTINUING THE SEQUENCE

Place numbers in the blank spaces to continue the sequence.

Example: 12   14   16   18   **20**   **22**   **24**

A–112   2   4   6   ____   ____   ____   ____

A–113   3   6   9   12   ____   ____   ____

A–114   5   10   15   ____   ____   ____   ____

A–115   24   26   28   30   ____   ____   ____

A–116   40   50   60   ____   ____   ____

A–117   30   35   40   ____   ____   ____   ____

A–118   30   33   36   ____   ____   ____   ____

COMPLETING THE SEQUENCE

Place numbers in the blank spaces to complete the sequence.

Example:	8	__**10**__	12	14	16	__**18**__	__**20**__

A–119   3   ____   9   12   ____   18

A–120   5   10   ____   ____   25   ____   ____

A–121   ____   ____   ____   30   ____   40   45   50

A–122   2   ____   6   ____   10   ____   14   16

A–123   ____   ____   19   ____   ____   22   23   24

A–124   ____   16   14   ____   10   ____   6   4

A–125   55   50   ____   ____   35   ____   ____

WHICH NUMBER BELONGS?

Each set contains five numbers.
The numbers have something in common.
Circle another number that belongs to the set.

Example: { 10, 30, 40, 20, 60 }   a. 45   b. 8

                                                     c. (50)   d. 17

A–126   { 5, 25, 10, 15, 20 }   a. 18   b. 30

                                                     c. 12   d. 1

A–127   { 64, 68, 63, 65, 60 }   a. 70   b. 6

                                                     c. 67   d. 54

A–128   { 8, 18, 14, 6, 12 }   a. 19   b. 4

                                                     c. 5   d. 21

A–129   { 3, 2, 9, 5, 6 }   a. 10   b. 7

                                                     c. 12   d. 23

WHICH NUMBER DOES NOT BELONG?

Each set contains five numbers.
Four of the numbers have something in common.
Circle the number in each set that does not belong.

Example: { 2, 6, 4, (7,) 8 }

A–130   { 10, 30, 46, 20, 50 }

A–131   { 25, 15, 45, 21, 35 }

A–132   { 75, 74, 71, 33, 79 }

A–133   { 12, 49, 32, 62, 42 }

A–134   { 33, 44, 21, 77, 55 }

A–135   { 1, 6, 3, 9, 7 }

A–136   { 5, 1, 2, 64, 6 }

MORE THAN

Shade all the rectangles that have more than 10 squares.

Example:

A–137

A–138

A–139

A–140

A–141

A–142

A–143

P.O. BOX 448, PACIFIC GROVE, CA 93950

LESS THAN

Shade all the rectangles that have less than 10 squares.

Example:

A–144

A–145

A–146

A–147

A–148

A–149

A–150

COMPARING SIZES OF SETS

Compare set A with set B.
Circle the set that contains more dots.

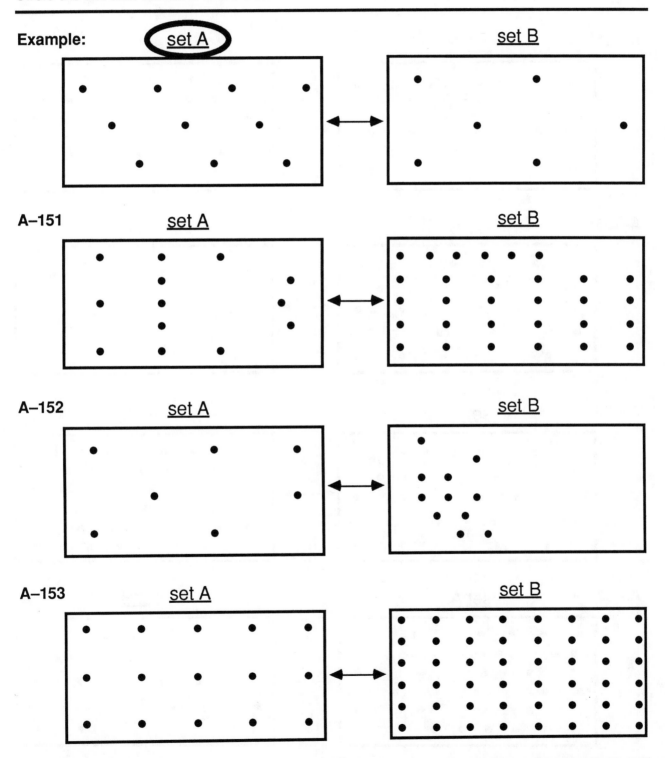

COMPARING SIZES OF SETS

Compare set A with set B.
Circle the set that contains more dots.

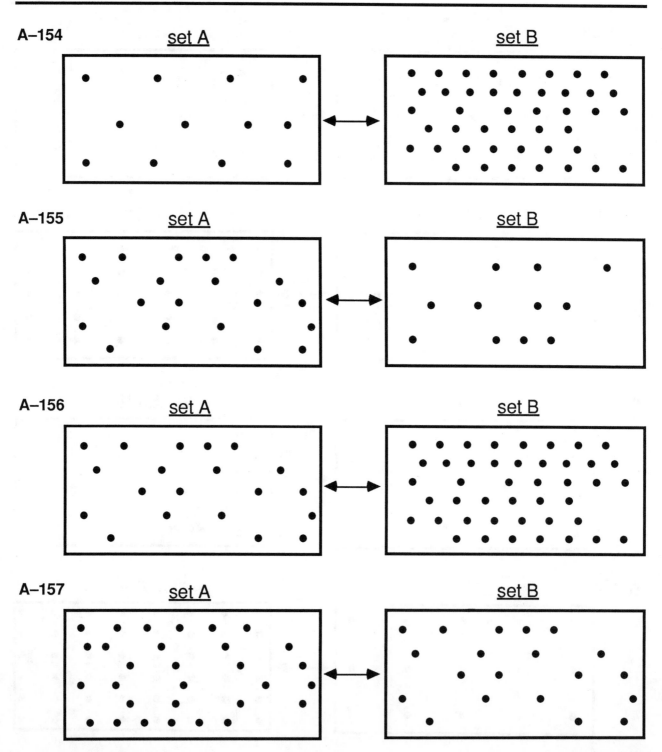

COMPARING SIZES OF SETS

Match the sets that have the same number of dots.

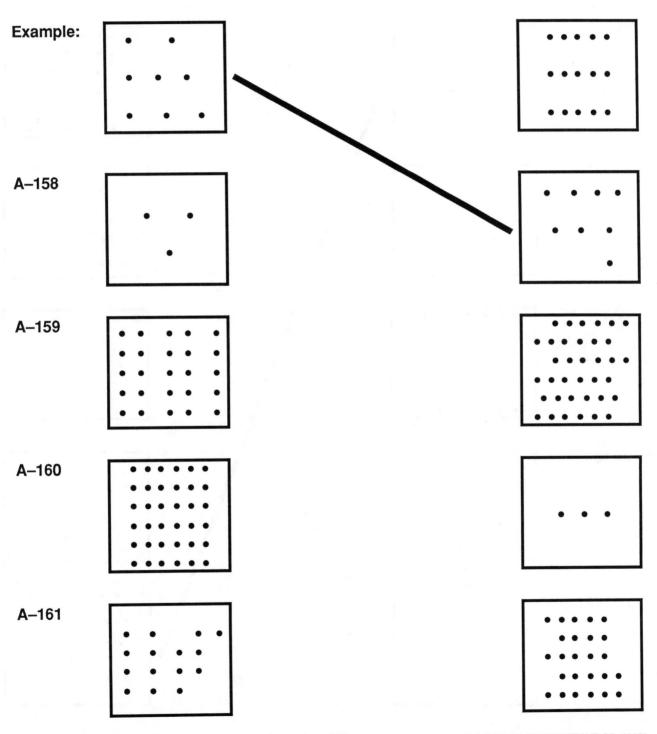

P.O. BOX 448, PACIFIC GROVE, CA 93950

COMPARING SIZES OF SETS

Match the sets that have almost the same number of dots.

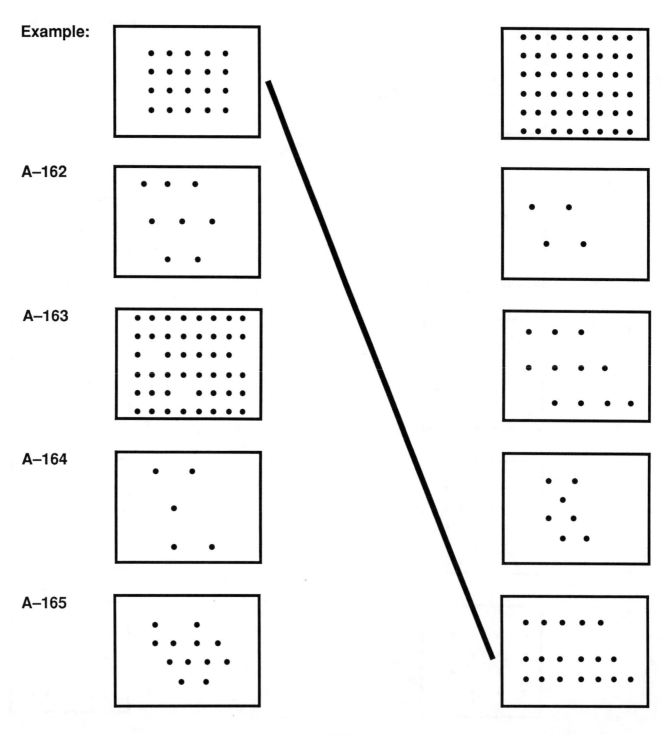

Example:

A–162

A–163

A–164

A–165

COUNTING PARTS

Count the number of shaded pieces in each circle.
Count the total number of pieces in each circle.
Write the answers in the boxes.

Example:

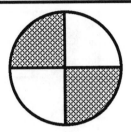

Shaded = 2

Total = 4

A–166

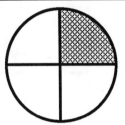

Shaded = ☐

Total = ☐

A–167

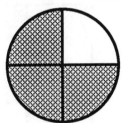

Shaded = ☐

Total = ☐

A–168

Shaded = ☐

Total = ☐

A–169

Shaded = ☐

Total = ☐

A–170

Shaded = ☐

Total = ☐

P.O. BOX 448, PACIFIC GROVE, CA 93950

COUNTING PARTS

Count the number of shaded squares in each figure.
Count the total number of squares in each figure.
Write the answers in the boxes.

A–171

Shaded = ☐

Total = ☐

A–172

Shaded = ☐

Total = ☐

A–173

Shaded = ☐

Total = ☐

A–174

Shaded = ☐

Total = ☐

A–175

Shaded = ☐

Total = ☐

A–176

Shaded = ☐

Total = ☐

MORE OR LESS THAN 1/2

Look at the shaded pieces in each circle.
If more than 1/2 of the circle is shaded, place an ✕ in the More box.
If less than 1/2 of the circle is shaded, place an ✕ in the Less box.

Example:

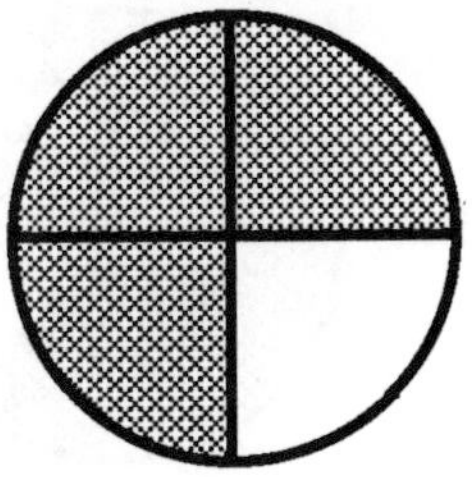

More ✕

Less

A–177

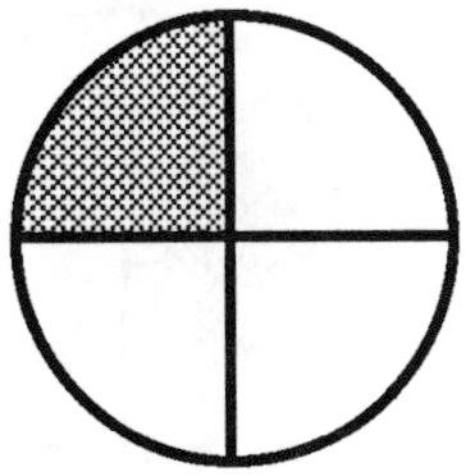

More

Less

A–178

More

Less

A–179

More

Less

A–180

More

Less

A–181

More

Less

P.O. BOX 448, PACIFIC GROVE, CA 93950

MORE OR LESS THAN 1/2

Look at the shaded part of each circle.
If more than 1/2 of the circle is shaded, place an ✕ in the More box.
If less than 1/2 of the circle is shaded, place an ✕ in the Less box.

Example:

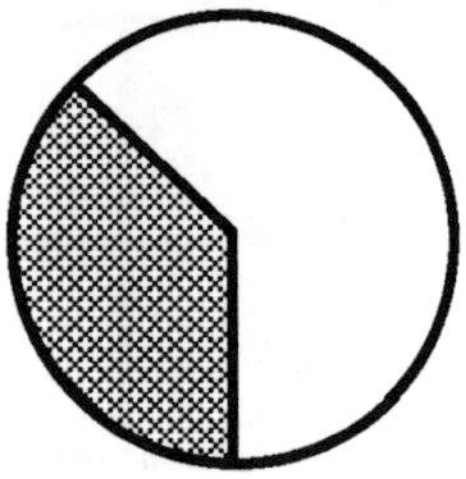

More ☐

Less ☒

A–182

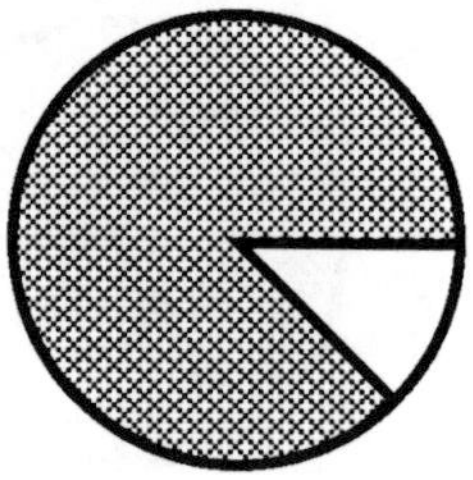

More ☐

Less ☐

A–183

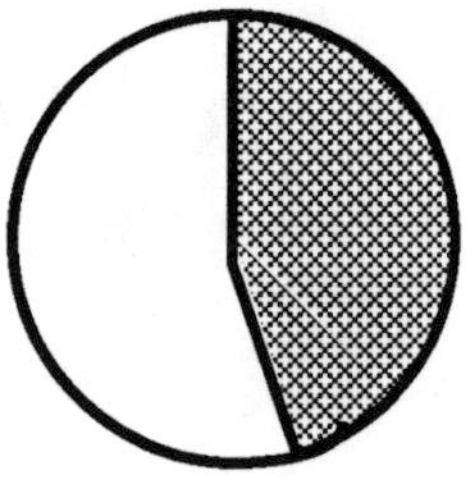

More ☐

Less ☐

A–184

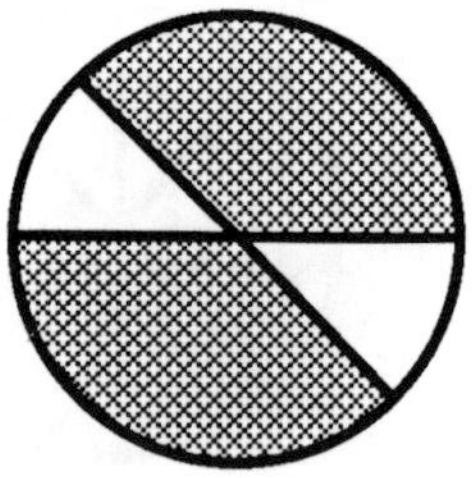

More ☐

Less ☐

A–185

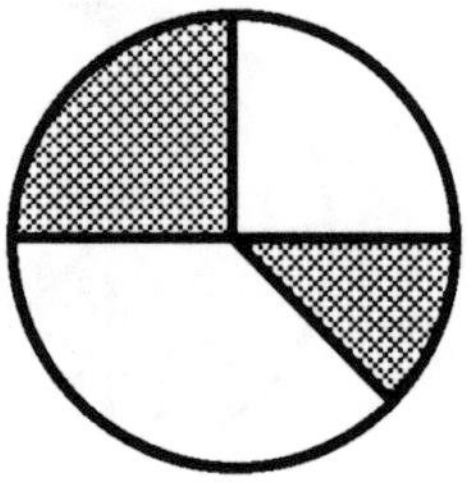

More ☐

Less ☐

A–186

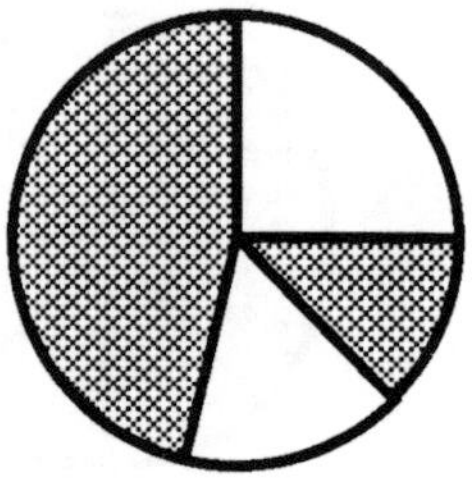

More ☐

Less ☐

POINTS ON THE NUMBER LINE

Some numbers are missing on each number line.
Write the missing numbers in the boxes.

Example:

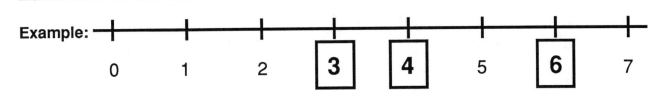

0   1   2   **3**   **4**   5   **6**   7

A–187

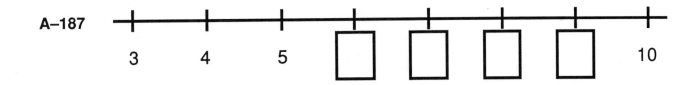

3   4   5   ☐   ☐   ☐   ☐   10

A–188

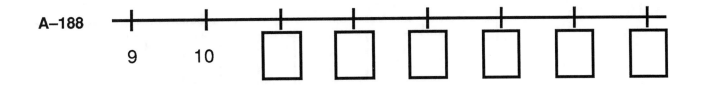

9   10   ☐   ☐   ☐   ☐   ☐   ☐

A–189

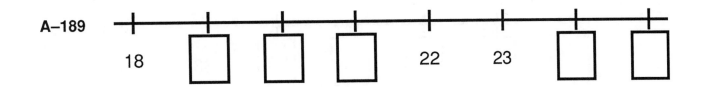

18   ☐   ☐   ☐   22   23   ☐   ☐

A–190

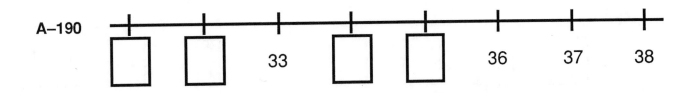

☐   ☐   33   ☐   ☐   36   37   38

                                       P.O. BOX 448, PACIFIC GROVE, CA 93950

POINTS ON THE NUMBER LINE

Some numbers are missing on each number line.
Write the missing numbers in the boxes.

A–191

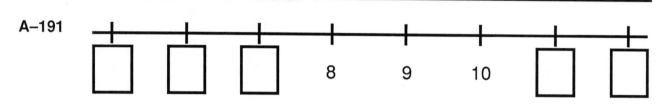

A–192

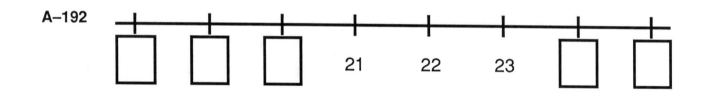

A–193

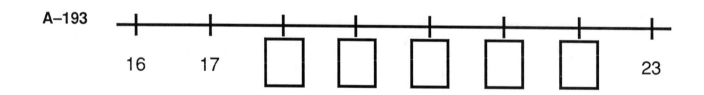

A–194

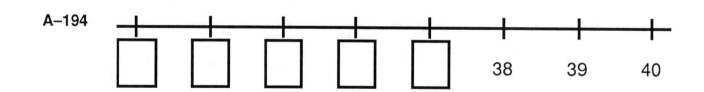

A–195

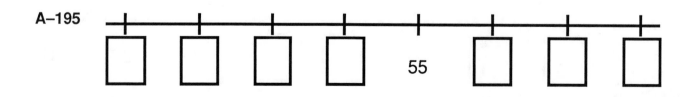

P.O. BOX 448, PACIFIC GROVE, CA 93950

WHAT IS THE NUMBER?

Look at the numbers on the number line.
The arrow is pointing to a missing number.
Write the missing number in the box.

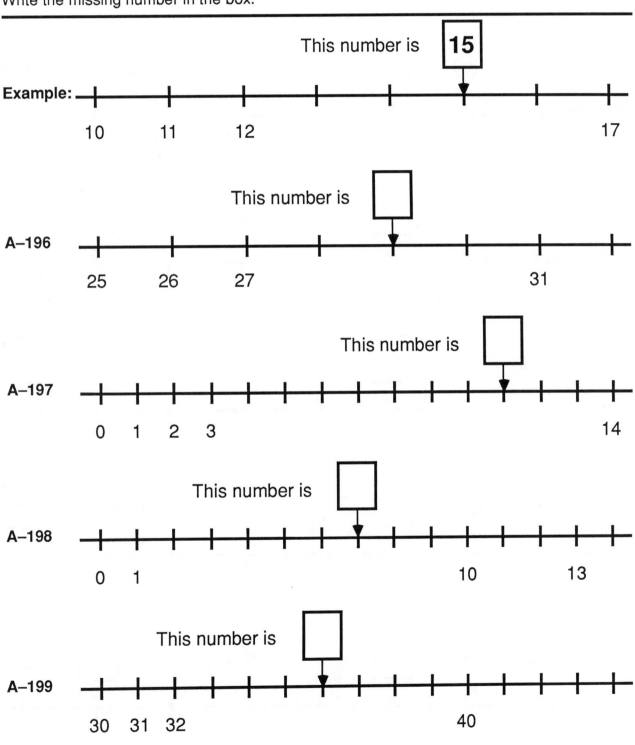

This number is **15**

Example:

10   11   12   17

This number is ☐

A–196

25   26   27   31

This number is ☐

A–197

0 1 2 3   14

This number is ☐

A–198

0 1   10   13

This number is ☐

A–199

30 31 32   40

35   P.O. BOX 448, PACIFIC GROVE, CA 93950

WHAT IS THE NUMBER?

One number is written in a box on each number line.
Write the missing number in the other box.

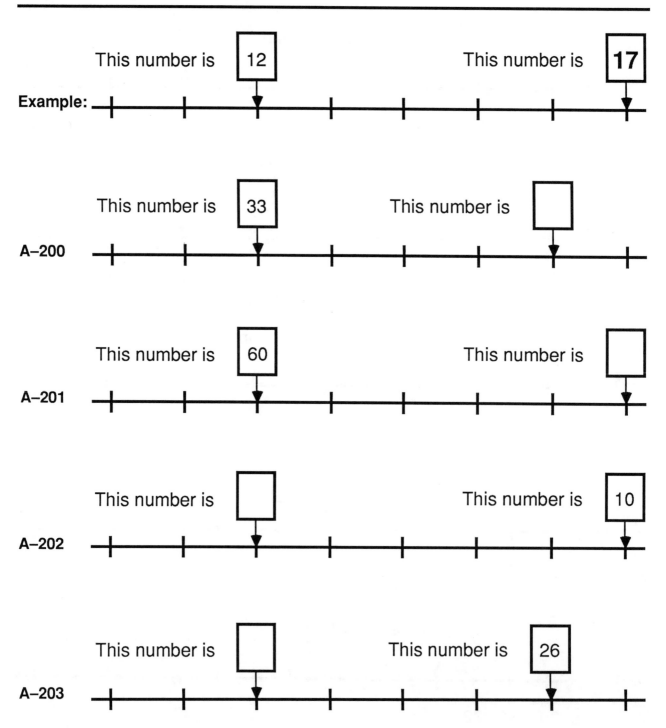

NAMING POINTS ON THE NUMBER LINE

Look at the set of four numbers above each number line.
Write each number in the correct box on the number line.

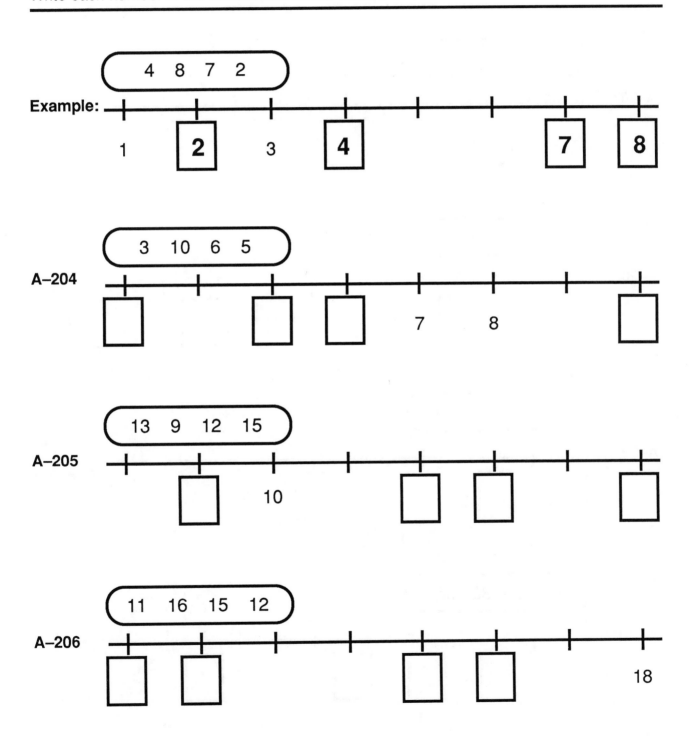

          P.O. BOX 448, PACIFIC GROVE, CA 93950

NAMING POINTS ON THE NUMBER LINE

Look at the set of four numbers above each number line.
Write each number in the correct box on the number line.

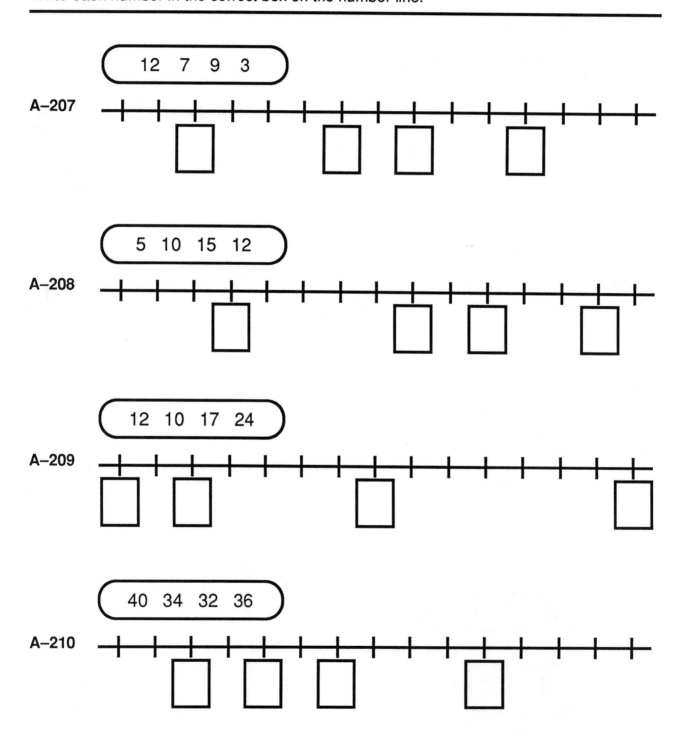

WHICH NUMBER DOES NOT FIT?

A part of the number line is shown.
Circle the number that does not fit on that part of the number line.

Example:

5   8   13

a. 6   b. 8
c. 10   d. (14)

A–211

9 10   17

a. 10   b. 12
c. 7   d. 16

A–212

10   19

a. 17   b. 21
c. 14   d. 12

A–213

23   28   31

a. 21   b. 28
c. 30   d. 24

A–214

48   56

a. 50   b. 49
c. 58   d. 53

A–215

65   73

a. 70   b. 69
c. 72   d. 60

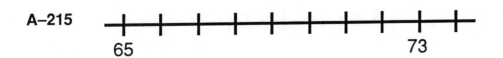
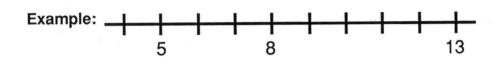

WHICH NUMBER DOES NOT FIT?

A part of the number line is shown.
Circle all the numbers that do not fit on that part of the number line.

Example: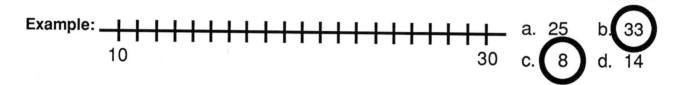

a. 25   b. 33

10   30   c. 8   d. 14

A–216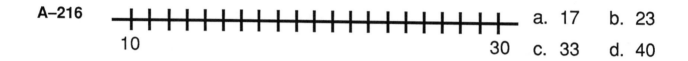

a. 17   b. 23

10   30   c. 33   d. 40

A–217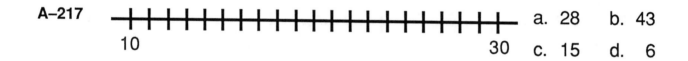

a. 28   b. 43

10   30   c. 15   d. 6

A–218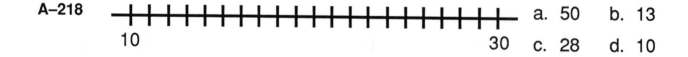

a. 50   b. 13

10   30   c. 28   d. 10

A–219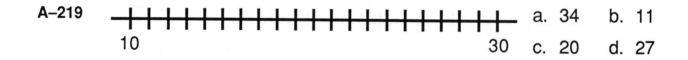

a. 34   b. 11

10   30   c. 20   d. 27

A–220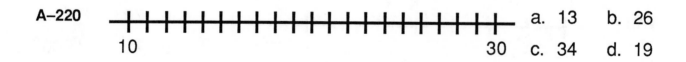

a. 13   b. 26

10   30   c. 34   d. 19

P.O. BOX 448, PACIFIC GROVE, CA 93950

WHICH IS NEAREST?

Look at the number in the box.
Circle the number in the row that is nearest to that number on the number line.

Example:	7 →	4	2	1	10	**(8)**
A–221	4 →	1	8	5	7	2
A–222	10 →	7	15	8	11	4
A–223	6 →	14	8	3	10	1
A–224	12 →	6	14	8	16	9
A–225	25 →	30	20	29	27	19

P.O. BOX 448, PACIFIC GROVE, CA 93950

WHICH IS NEAREST?

Look at the number in the box.
Circle the number in the row that is nearest to that number on the number line.

A–226 | 5 ⟶ | 3   7   4   9   8

A–227 | 10 ⟶ | 6   12   7   14   18

A–228 | 14 ⟶ | 11   17   16   10   9

A–229 | 9 ⟶ | 6   14   12   16   7

A–230 | 23 ⟶ | 19   25   28   20   26

A–231 | 59 ⟶ | 56   61   64   55   49

P.O. BOX 448, PACIFIC GROVE, CA 93950

GREATER THAN

Circle all the numbers in the box that are greater than the number in the square.
Put an ✗ on the largest number in each box.

Example:

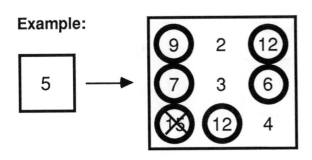

A–232

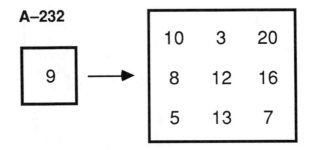

A–233

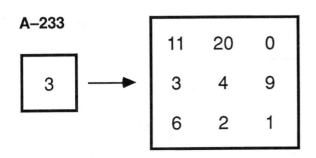

A–234

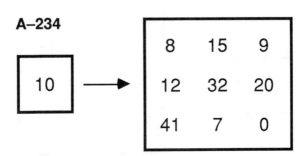

A–235

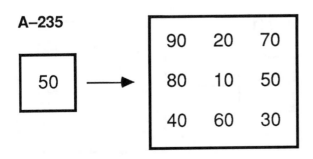

A–236

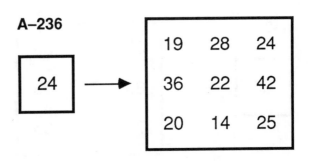

43   P.O. BOX 448, PACIFIC GROVE, CA 93950

LESS THAN

Circle all the numbers in the box that are less than the number in the square.
Put an X on the smallest number in each box.

Example:

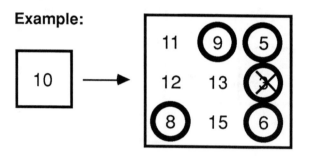

A–237

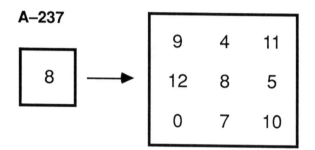

A–238

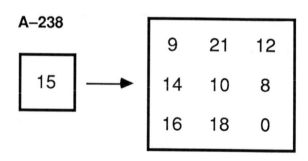

A–239

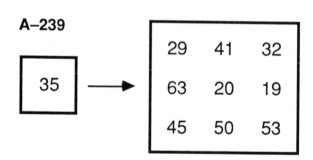

A–240

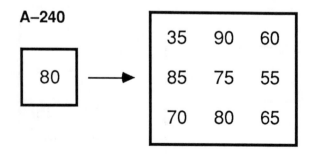

A–241

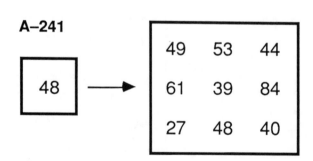

44   P.O. BOX 448, PACIFIC GROVE, CA 93950

BETWEEN

Circle all the numbers in the box that are between the two numbers above the box.

Example: <u>2 and 6</u>

④	10	⑤
8	0	③
9	1	7

A–242   <u>3 and 7</u>

6	9	5
1	8	2
4	10	7

A–243   <u>4 and 8</u>

7	9	8
3	6	4
6	10	7

A–244   <u>5 and 11</u>

4	15	9
7	17	2
6	12	10

A–245   <u>10 and 15</u>

12	20	5
16	9	14
10	8	13

A–246   <u>23 and 32</u>

19	28	23
30	33	27
21	31	32

BETWEEN

Circle all the numbers in the box that are between the two numbers above the box.

A–247   13 and 16

10	11	12
13	14	15
16	17	18

A–248   13 and 18

18	16	21
14	12	11
19	17	23

A–249   20 and 30

15	35	10
45	20	30
25	5	40

A–250   15 and 35

65	0	25
15	50	30
60	10	20

A–251   55 and 70

72	49	68
59	71	80
81	54	27

A–252   34 and 45

39	28	46
34	43	54
41	30	35

46   P.O. BOX 448, PACIFIC GROVE, CA 93950

USING PLACE VALUE TO MATCH SETS

Each rod is made with 10 cubes.
Draw a line around groups of 10 cubes in the sets in the first column.
Match these sets with the same number of cubes in the second column.

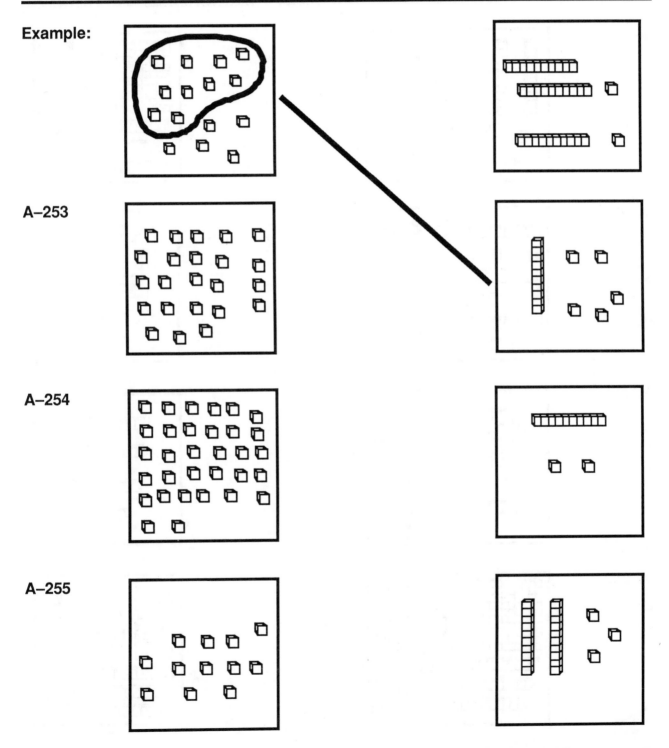

Example:

A–253

A–254

A–255

USING PLACE VALUE TO MATCH SETS

Each flat is made with 100 cubes. Each rod is made with 10 cubes.
Draw a line around groups of 10 cubes in the sets in the first column.
Match these sets with the same number of cubes in the second column.

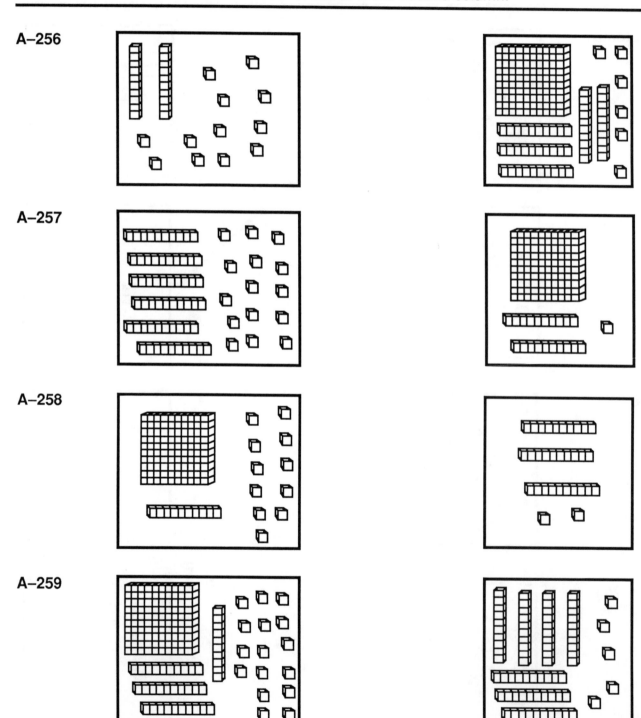

A–256

A–257

A–258

A–259

COUNTING RODS AND CUBES

Match each set with the chart that shows how many rods and cubes are in the set.

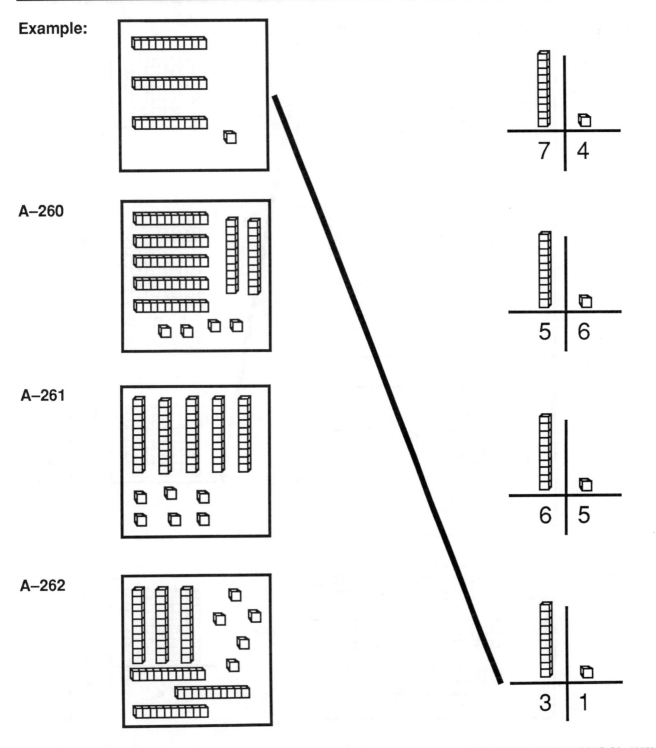

COUNTING FLATS, RODS, AND CUBES

Match each set with the chart that shows how many flats, rods, and cubes are in the set.

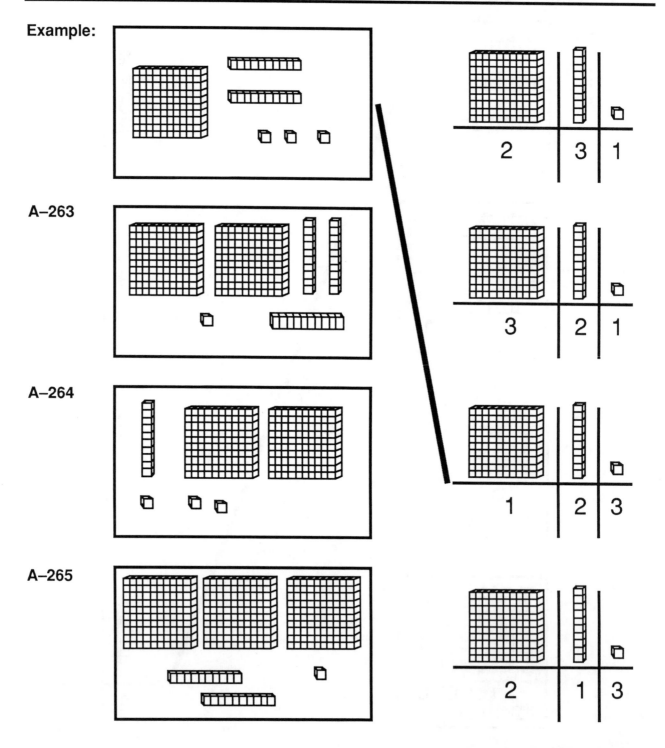

COUNTING RODS AND CUBES

Each rod is made with 10 cubes.
Write the number of rods and cubes in the chart.
Write the total number of cubes in the circle.

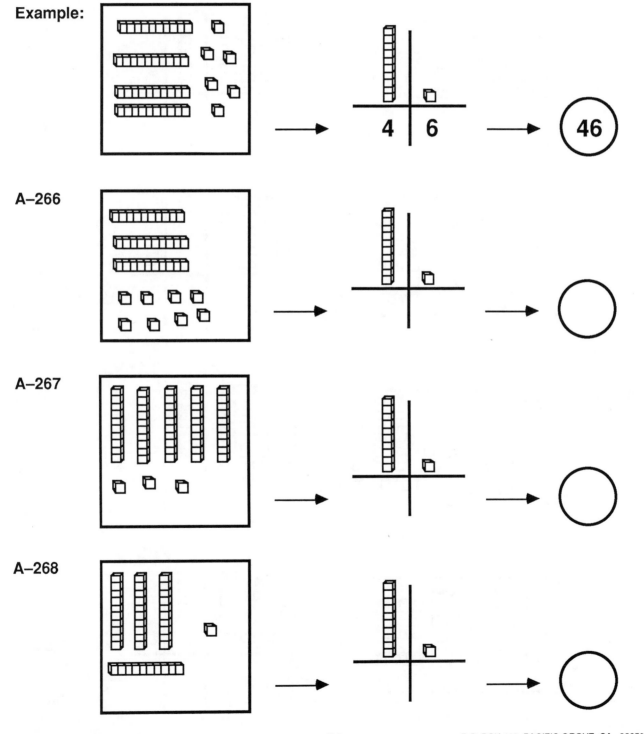

Example:

A–266

A–267

A–268

COUNTING FLATS, RODS, AND CUBES

Each flat is made with 100 cubes. Each rod is made with 10 cubes.
Write the number of flats, rods, and cubes in the chart.
Write the total number of cubes in the circle.

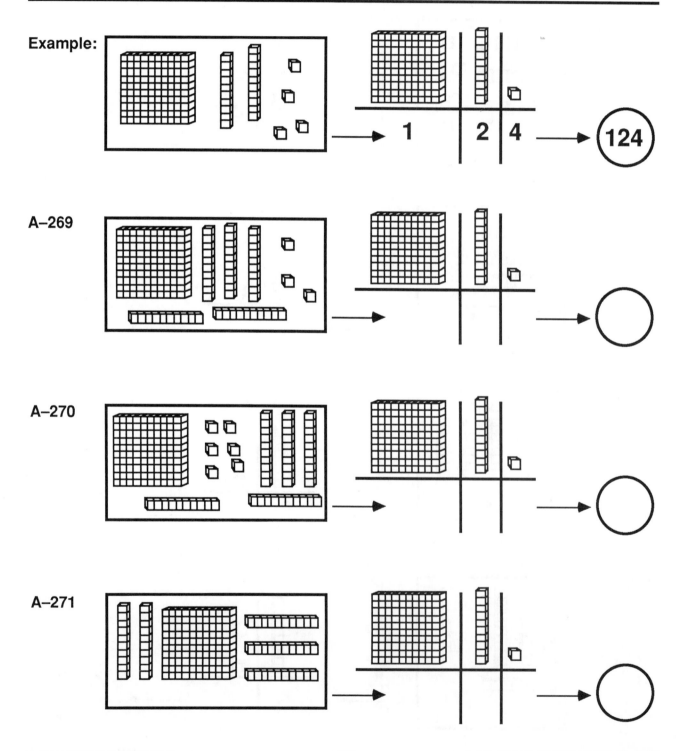

COUNTING RODS AND CUBES

Each rod is made with 10 cubes.
Match each set with the correct number.

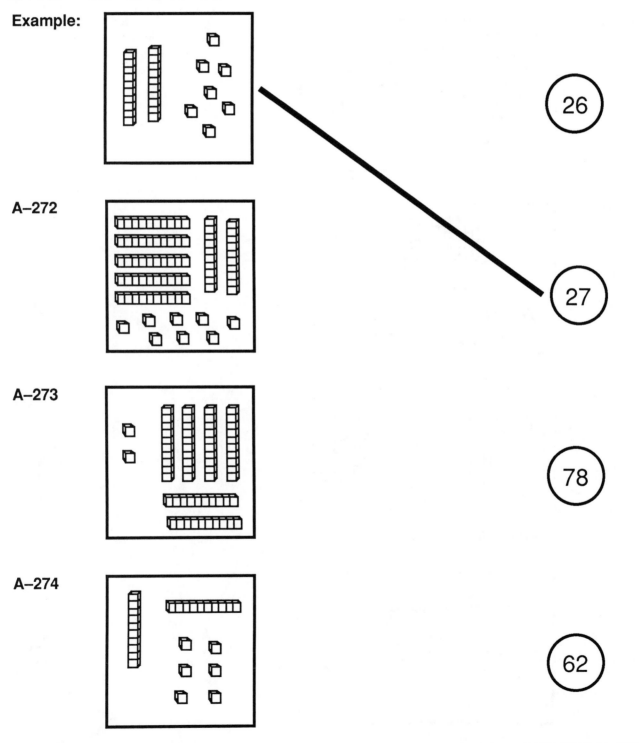

Example:

A–272

A–273

A–274

26

27

78

62

COUNTING FLATS, RODS, AND CUBES

Each flat is made with 100 cubes. Each rod is made with 10 cubes.
Match each set with its correct number.

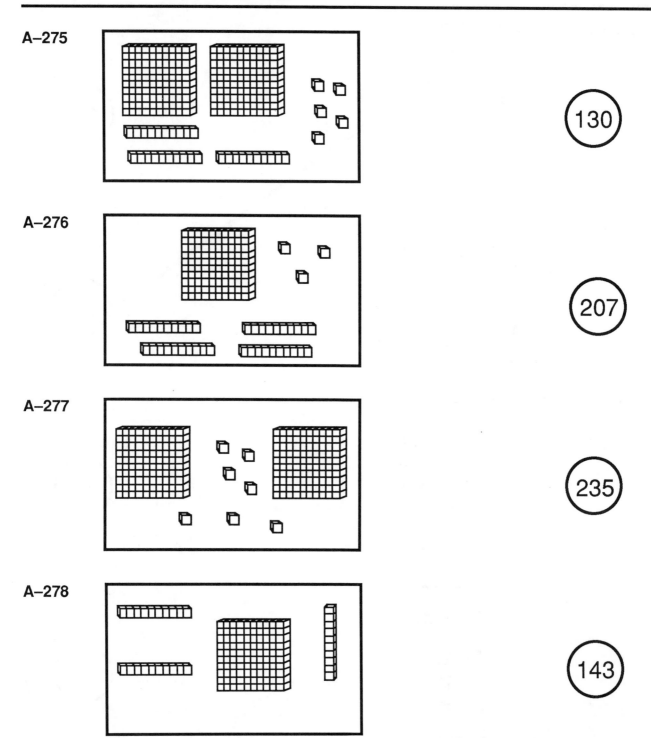

A–275

A–276

A–277

A–278

130

207

235

143

P.O. BOX 448, PACIFIC GROVE, CA 93950

COUNTING RODS AND CUBES

Each rod is made with 10 cubes.
Put an ✕ on the rods and cubes that are needed to make the number in the circle.

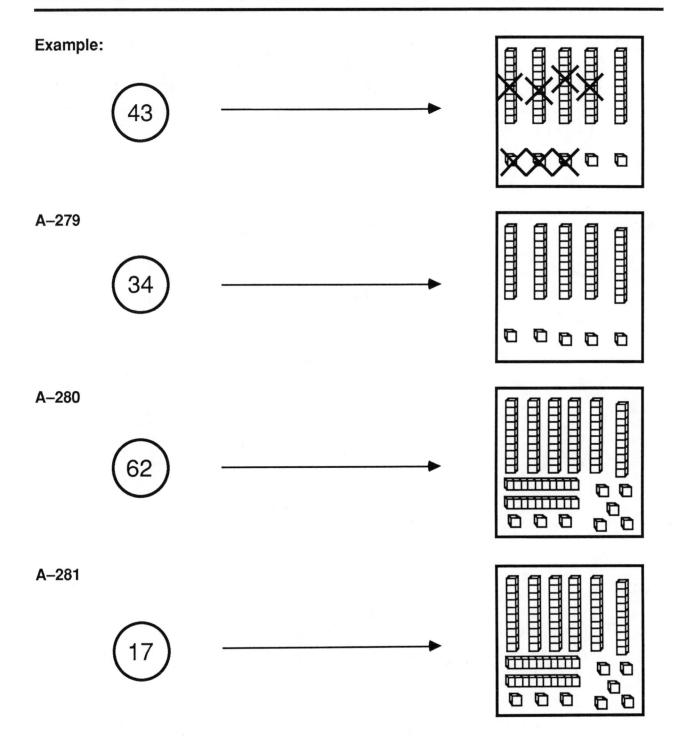

Example:

A–279

A–280

A–281

COUNTING FLATS, RODS, AND CUBES

Each flat is made with 100 cubes. Each rod is made with 10 cubes.
Put an ✕ on the flats, rods, and cubes that are needed to make the number in the circle.

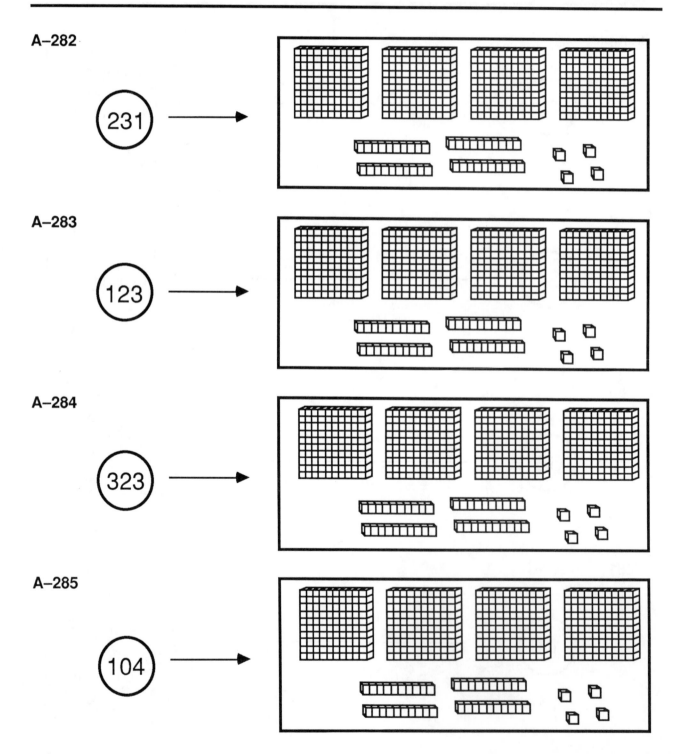

A–282

231

A–283

123

A–284

323

A–285

104

COUNTING RODS AND CUBES

Each rod is made with 10 cubes.
Write the number of rods and cubes in the chart.
Write the total number of cubes in the circle.

Example:

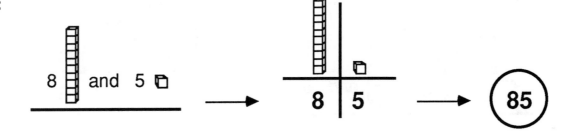

A–286

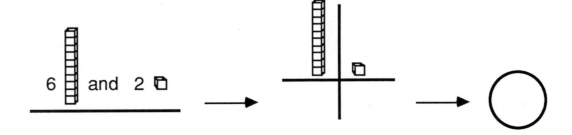

A–287

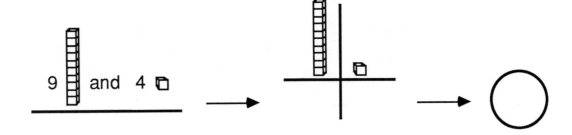

A–288

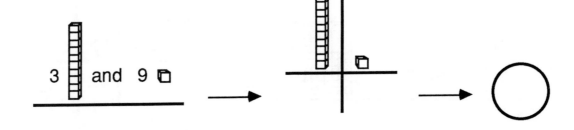

COUNTING FLATS, RODS, AND CUBES

Each flat is made with 100 cubes. Each rod is made with 10 cubes.
Write the number of flats, rods, and cubes in the chart.
Write the total number of cubes in the circle.

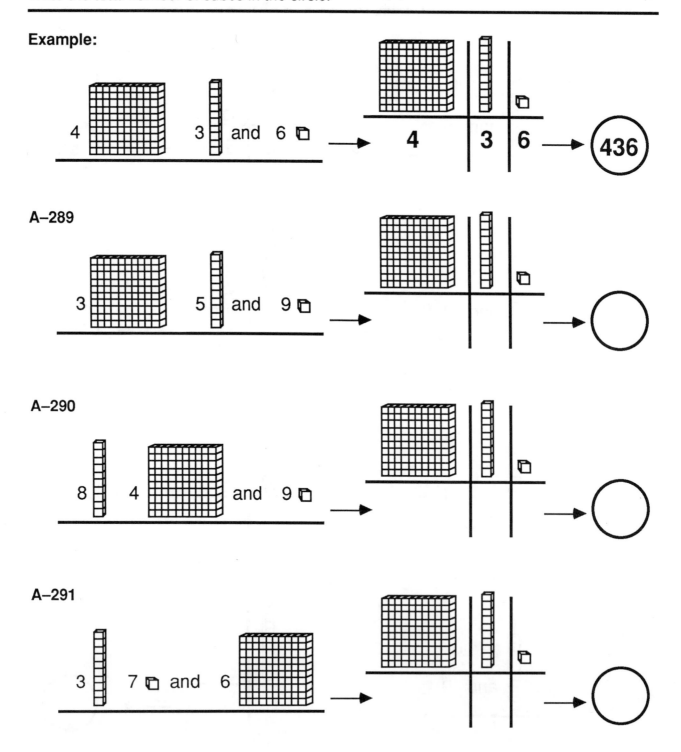

Example:

4   3 and 6 → | **4** | **3** | **6** | → (**436**)

A–289

3   5 and 9 →

A–290

8   4 and 9 →

A–291

3   7 and 6 →

COUNTING RODS AND CUBES

Each rod is made with 10 cubes.
Circle the number that shows the total number of cubes in each group.

Example: 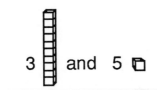 3 and 5

      a. 53
      b. (35)
      c. 33

A–292   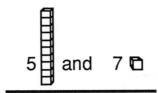 5 and 7

      a. 57
      b. 75
      c. 77

A–293   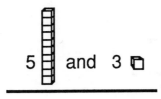 5 and 3

      a. 53
      b. 35
      c. 33

A–294   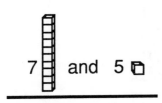 7 and 5

      a. 75
      b. 57
      c. 55

                   P.O. BOX 448, PACIFIC GROVE, CA 93950

COUNTING FLATS, RODS, AND CUBES

Each flat is made with 100 cubes. Each rod is made with 10 cubes.
Circle the number that shows the total number of cubes in each group.

Example:

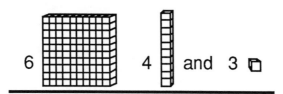

6   4 and 3

a. 436
b. (643)
c. 364

A–295

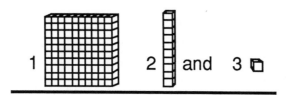

1   2 and 3

a. 321
b. 231
c. 123

A–296

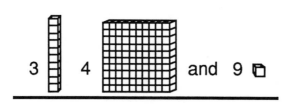

3   4 and 9

a. 439
b. 349
c. 943

A–297

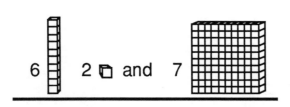

6   2 and 7

a. 267
b. 627
c. 762

                                      P.O. BOX 448, PACIFIC GROVE, CA 93950

COUNTING RODS AND CUBES

Each rod is made with 10 cubes.
Look at the number in each box.
Fill in the blanks to show how many rods and cubes are needed to make the number.

Example:

8 and **5**

A–298

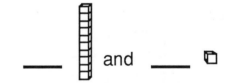

___ and ___

A–299

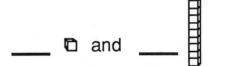

___ and ___

A–300

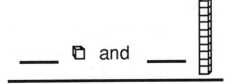

___ and ___

                   P.O. BOX 448, PACIFIC GROVE, CA 93950

COUNTING FLATS, RODS, AND CUBES

Each flat is made with 100 cubes. Each rod is made with 10 cubes.
Look at the number in the box.
Fill in the blanks to show how many flats, rods, and cubes are needed to make the number.

A–301

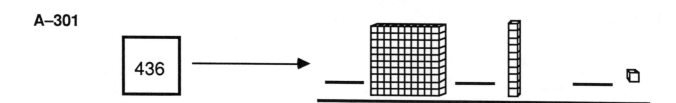

436

A–302

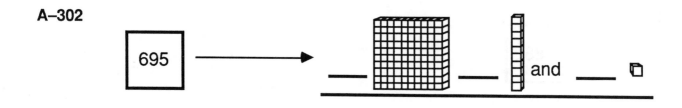

695

A–303

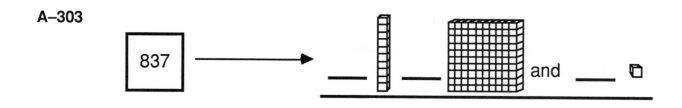

837

A–304

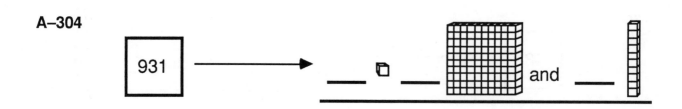

931

ESTIMATING LENGTH—LESS THAN

The shaded rectangle is 10 centimeters long.

Shade all the rectangles with lengths less than 10 centimeters.

Example:

B–1

B–2

B–3

B–4

B–5

B–6

B–7

ESTIMATING LENGTH—LESS THAN

The shaded rectangle is 10 centimeters long.

Shade all the rectangles with lengths less than 10 centimeters.

Example:

B–8

B–9

B–10

B–11

B–12

B–13

B–14

ESTIMATING LENGTH—GREATER THAN

The shaded rectangle is 5 centimeters long.

Shade all the rectangles with lengths greater than 5 centimeters.

Example:

B–15

B–16

B–17

B–18

B–19

B–20

B–21

P.O. BOX 448, PACIFIC GROVE, CA 93950

ESTIMATING LENGTH—GREATER THAN

The shaded rectangle is 5 centimeters long.

Shade all the rectangles with lengths greater than 5 centimeters.

Example:

B–22

B–23

B–24

B–25

B–26

B–27

B–28

66   P.O. BOX 448, PACIFIC GROVE, CA 93950

ESTIMATING LENGTH—BETWEEN

The dotted rectangle is 10 centimeters long.
The shaded rectangle is 5 centimeters long.

Shade all the rectangles with lengths between 5 centimeters and 10 centimeters.

Example:

B–29

B–30

B–31

B–32

B–33

B–34

P.O. BOX 448, PACIFIC GROVE, CA 93950

ESTIMATING LENGTH—BETWEEN

The dotted rectangle is 10 centimeters long.
The shaded rectangle is 5 centimeters long.

Shade all the rectangles with lengths between 5 centimeters and 10 centimeters.

Example:

B–35

B–36

B–37

B–38

B–39

B–40

68   P.O. BOX 448, PACIFIC GROVE, CA 93950

COMPARING LENGTHS

Put an ✗ on the longer line.

Example:

B–41

B–42

B–43

B–44

B–45

B–46   **B–47**   **B–48**   **B–49**

69   P.O. BOX 448, PACIFIC GROVE, CA 93950

COMPARING LENGTHS

Put an ✕ on the longest line.

Example:

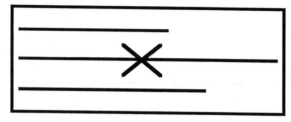

B–50

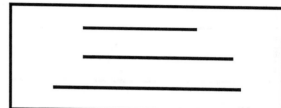

B–51

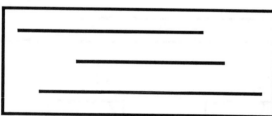

B–52

B–53

B–54

B–55

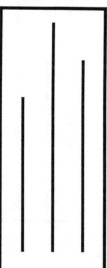

B–56

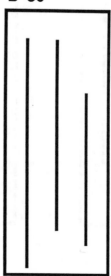

B–57

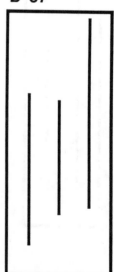

P.O. BOX 448, PACIFIC GROVE, CA 93950

COMPARING LENGTHS

Put an ✕ on the shorter line.

Example:

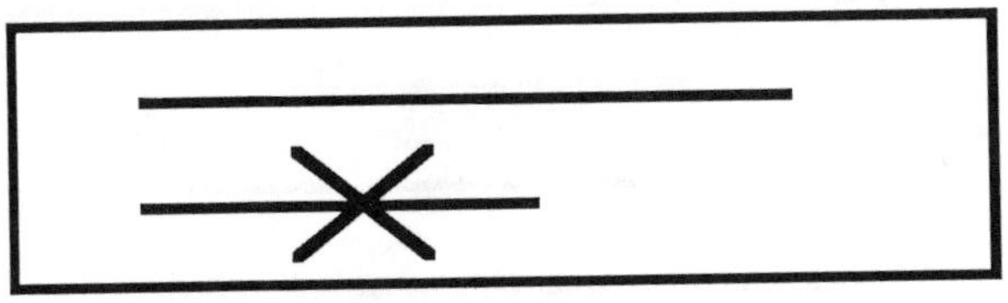

B–58

B–59

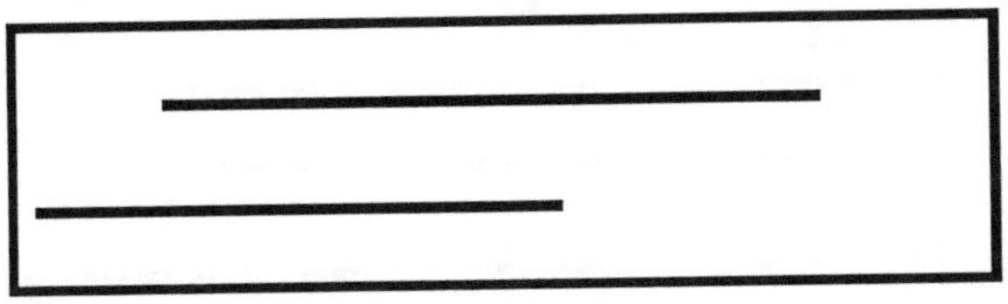

B–60

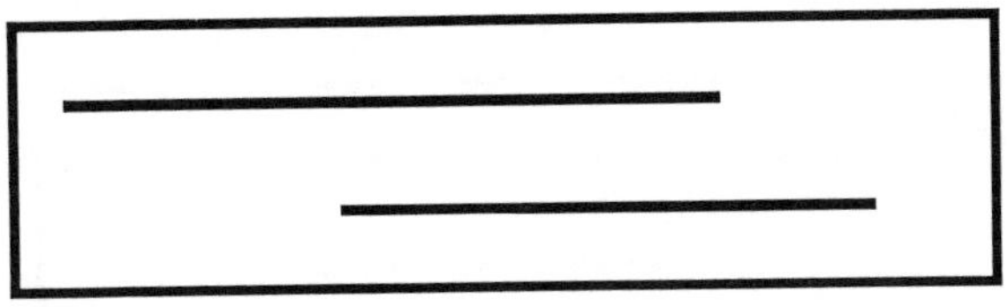

B–61

B–62

B–63 　　**B–64** 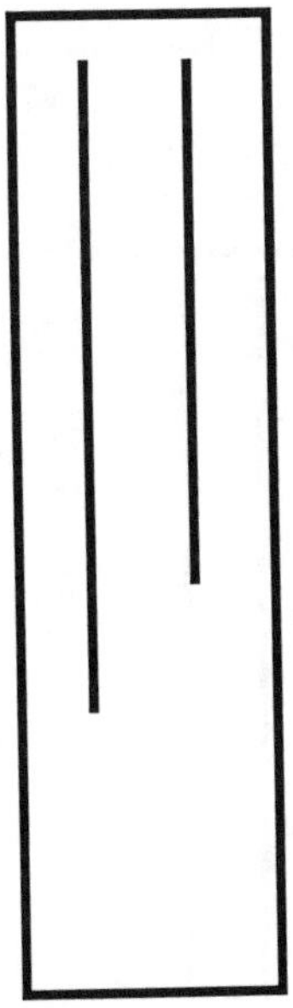　　**B–65** 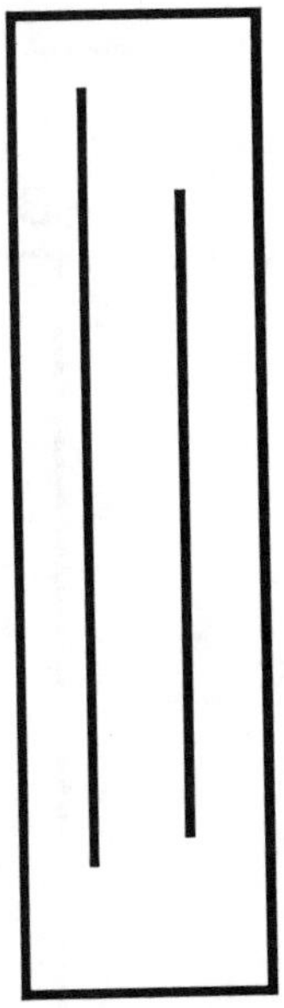　　**B–66**

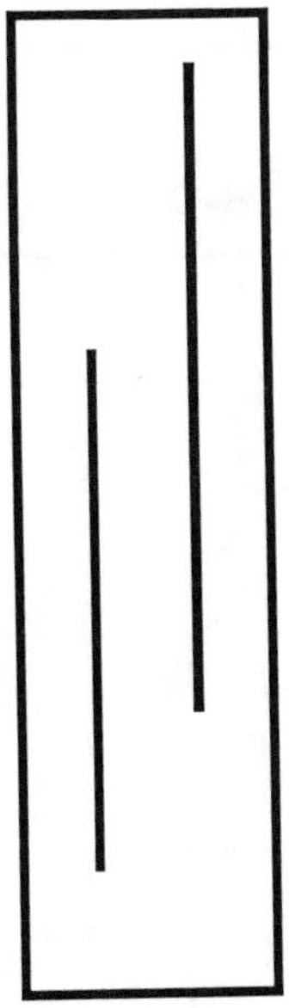

P.O. BOX 448, PACIFIC GROVE, CA 93950

COMPARING LENGTHS

Put an ✕ on the shortest line.

Example:

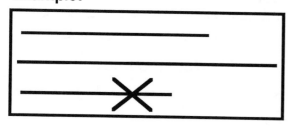

B–67

B–68

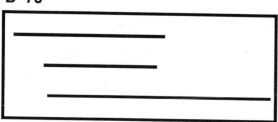

B–69

B–70

B–71

B–72

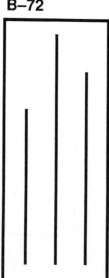

B–73

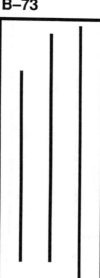

B–74

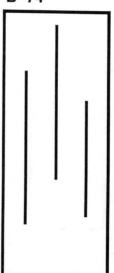

     72   P.O. BOX 448, PACIFIC GROVE, CA 93950

COMPARING LENGTHS

Put an ✕ on the shortest side of the shape.

Example:

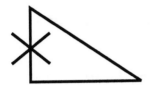

B–75

B–76

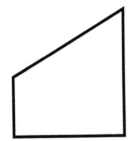

B–77

B–78

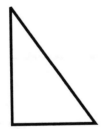

B–79

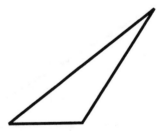

B–80

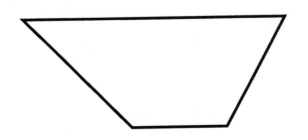

B–81

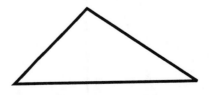

P.O. BOX 448, PACIFIC GROVE, CA 93950

COMPARING LENGTHS

Put an X on the shorter line.

Example:	**B–82**
B–83	**B–84**
B–85	**B–86**
B–87	**B–88**

COMPARING LENGTHS

Put an X on the longest side of the shape.

Example: **B–89**

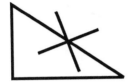   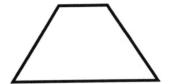

B–90   **B–91**

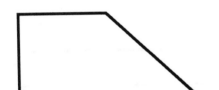   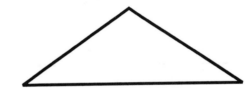

B–92   **B–93**

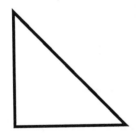   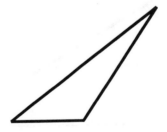

B–94   **B–95**

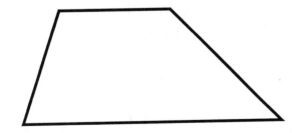   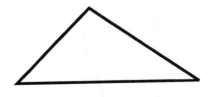

                             P.O. BOX 448, PACIFIC GROVE, CA 93950

COMPARING LENGTHS

Put an X on the longer line.

Example:

B–96

B–97

B–98

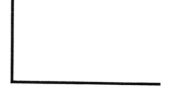

B–99

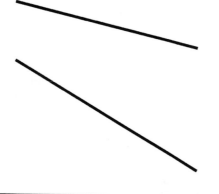

B–100

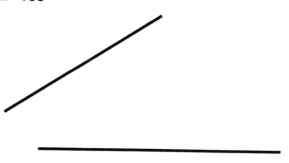

B–101

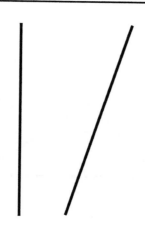

B–102

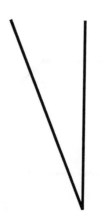

P.O. BOX 448, PACIFIC GROVE, CA 93950

CLASSIFYING BY SHAPE

Put an ✕ on the shapes that have three sides.

Example:

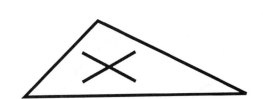

B–103

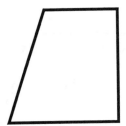

B–104

B–105

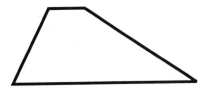

B–106

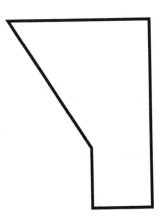

B–107

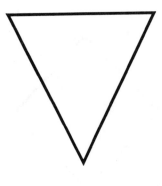

B–108

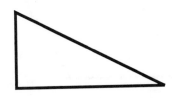

B–109

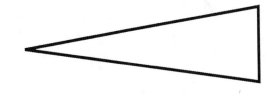

P.O. BOX 448, PACIFIC GROVE, CA 93950

CLASSIFYING BY SHAPE

Put an X on the shapes that have four sides.

Example:

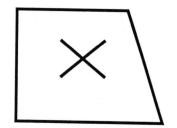

B–110

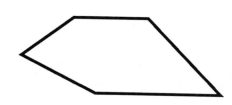

B–111

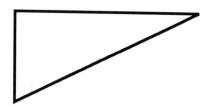

B–112

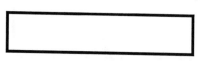

B–113

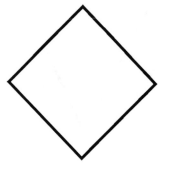

B–114

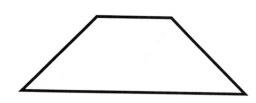

B–115

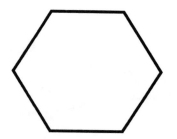

B–116

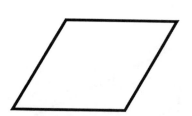

78   P.O. BOX 448, PACIFIC GROVE, CA 93950

CLASSIFYING BY SHAPE

Put an X on the shapes that have three sides <u>and</u> one square corner.

Example:

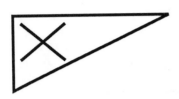

B–117

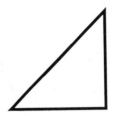

B–118

B–119

B–120

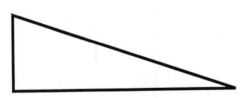

B–121

B–122

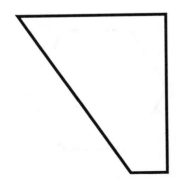

B–123

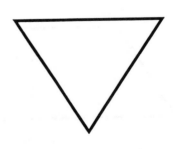

79

P.O. BOX 448, PACIFIC GROVE, CA 93950

CLASSIFYING BY SHAPE

Put an X on the shapes that have one <u>or</u> more square corners.

Example:

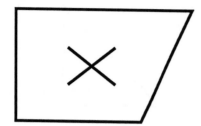

B–124

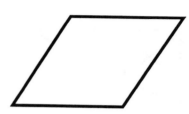

B–125

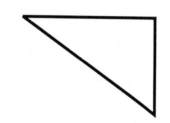

B–126

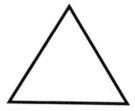

B–127

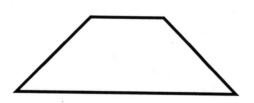

B–128

B–129

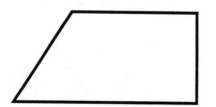

B–130

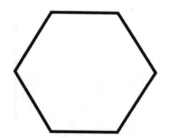

80   P.O. BOX 448, PACIFIC GROVE, CA 93950

CLASSIFYING BY SHAPE

Put an ✕ on the shape that belongs to the group in the box.

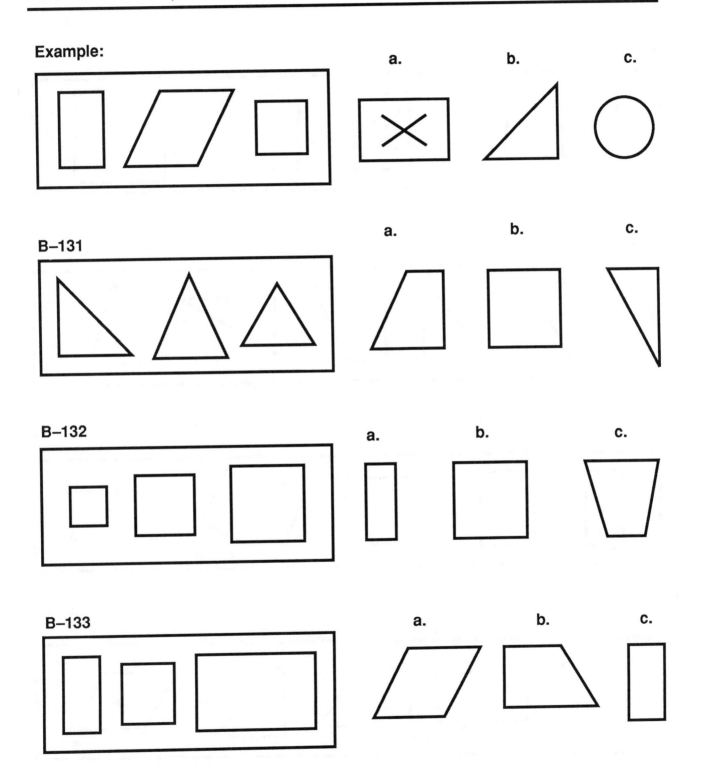

Example:

a.   b.   c.

B–131

a.   b.   c.

B–132

a.   b.   c.

B–133

a.   b.   c.

CLASSIFYING BY SHAPE

Put an ✕ on the shape that does not belong to the group in the box.

Example:

B–134

B–135

B–136

SYMMETRY

A shape is symmetric if you can fold it and the two halves match.
Draw dotted lines to show where to fold these symmetric figures.

Example:

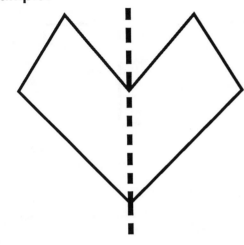

B–137

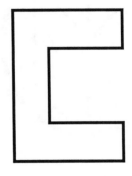

B–138

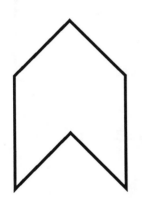

B–139

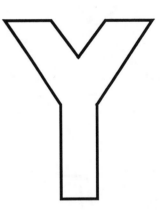

B–140

B–141

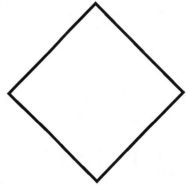

                                               P.O. BOX 448, PACIFIC GROVE, CA 93950

SYMMETRY

Draw a line around the symmetric figures.
Draw dotted lines to show where to fold the symmetric figures.

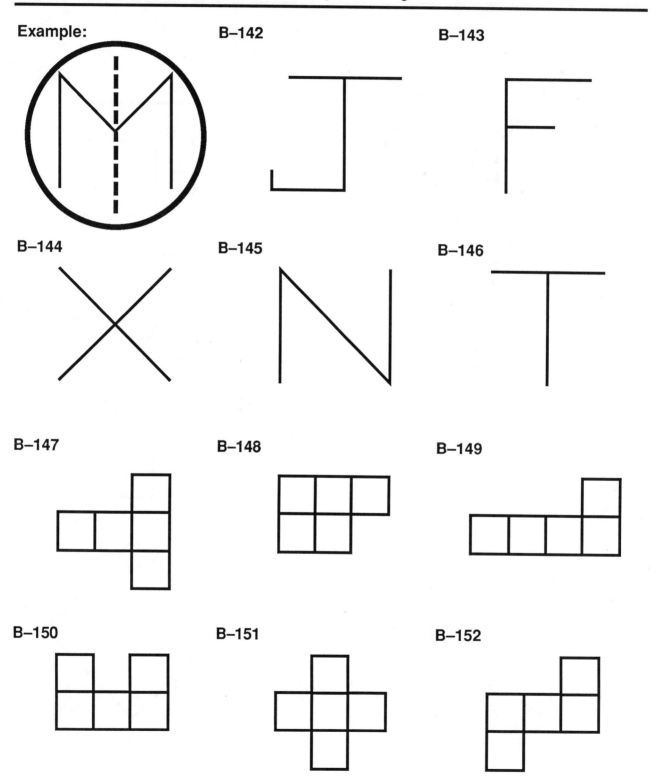

Example: **B–142**   **B–143**

B–144   **B–145**   **B–146**

B–147   **B–148**   **B–149**

B–150   **B–151**   **B–152**

SYMMETRY

The shaded shape is cut from the folded paper.
Draw the shape when the paper is opened.

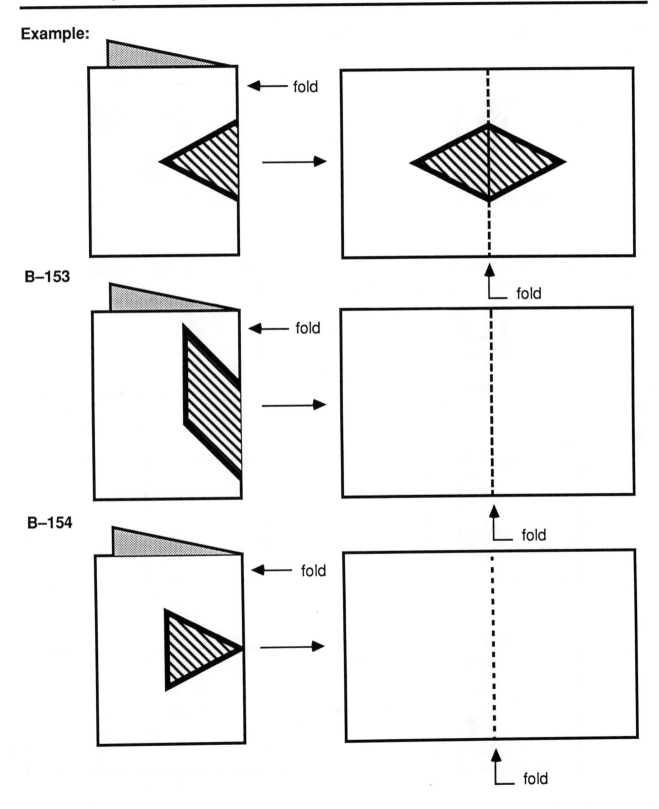

Example:

B–153

B–154

SYMMETRY

The shaded shape is cut from the folded paper.
Draw the letter that is made when the paper is opened.
Use the four letters to spell a word.

Example:

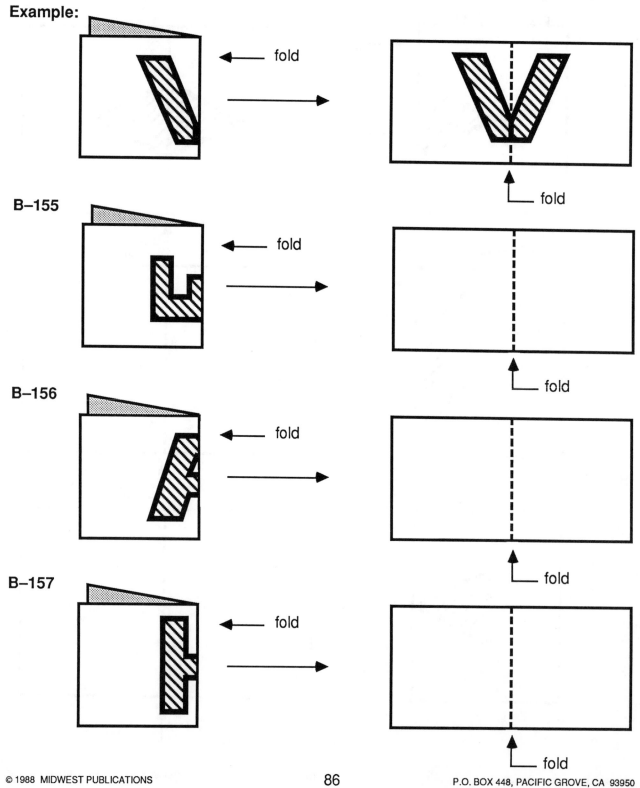

B–155

B–156

B–157

SYMMETRY

Draw a line around the symmetric figures.
Draw a dotted line to show where to fold the symmetric figures.

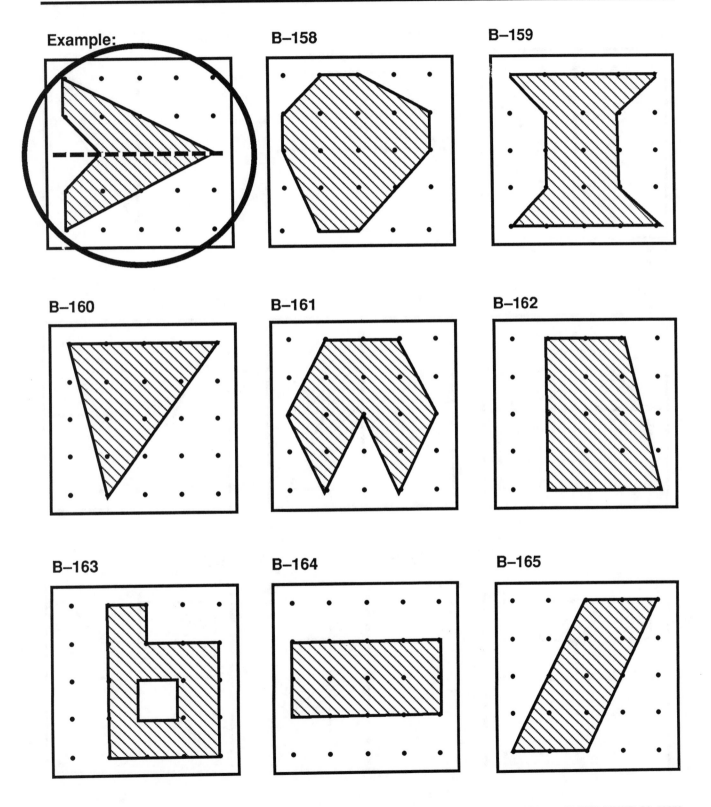

SYMMETRY

The dotted line shows the fold.
Draw the other half of each symmetric figure.

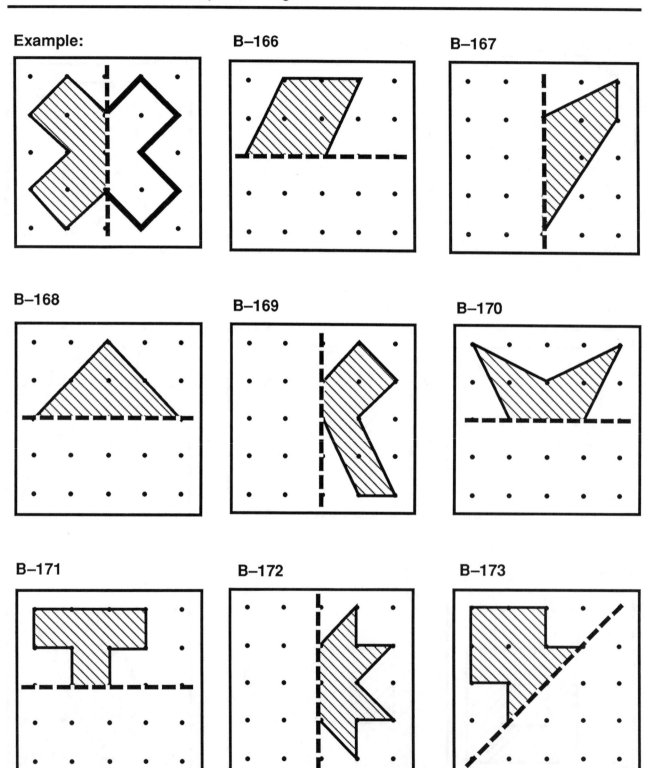

Example:

B–166

B–167

B–168

B–169

B–170

B–171

B–172

B–173

MOTIONS—SLIDES

If you slide triangle 1 across the page you get triangle 2.

Write a 2 in the shape that shows a slide.

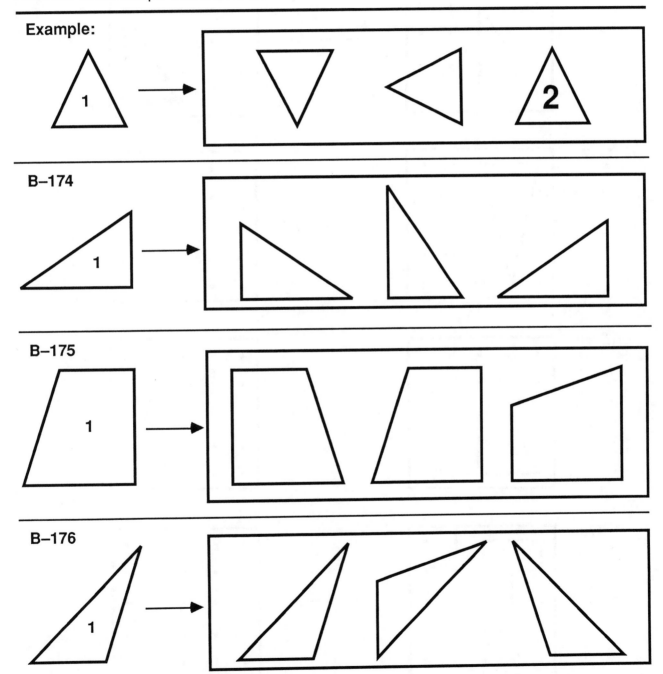

Example:

B–174

B–175

B–176

MOTIONS—SLIDES

A figure is pictured before a slide.
The slide is two dots to the right.
Draw the picture after the slide.

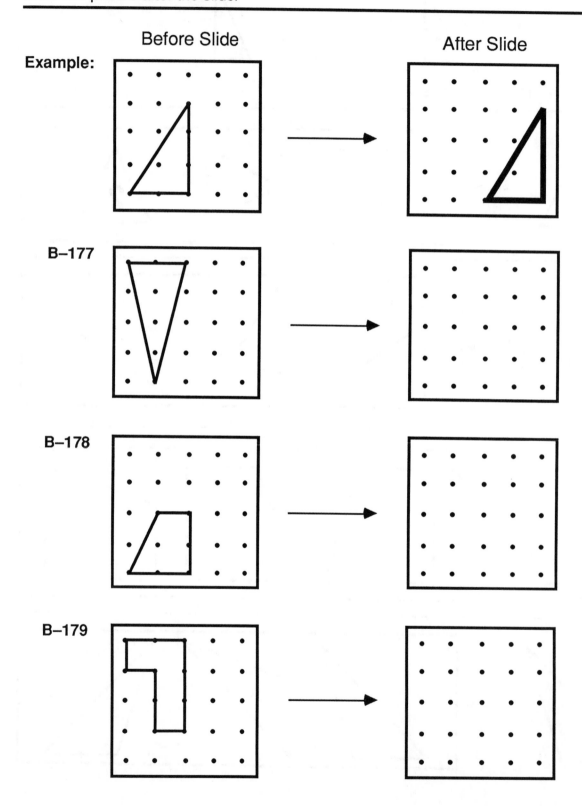

Before Slide   After Slide

Example:

B–177

B–178

B–179

MOTIONS—FLIPS

If you flip over triangle 1 you get triangle 2.

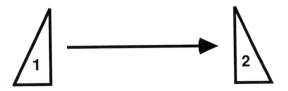

Write a 2 in the shape that shows a flip.

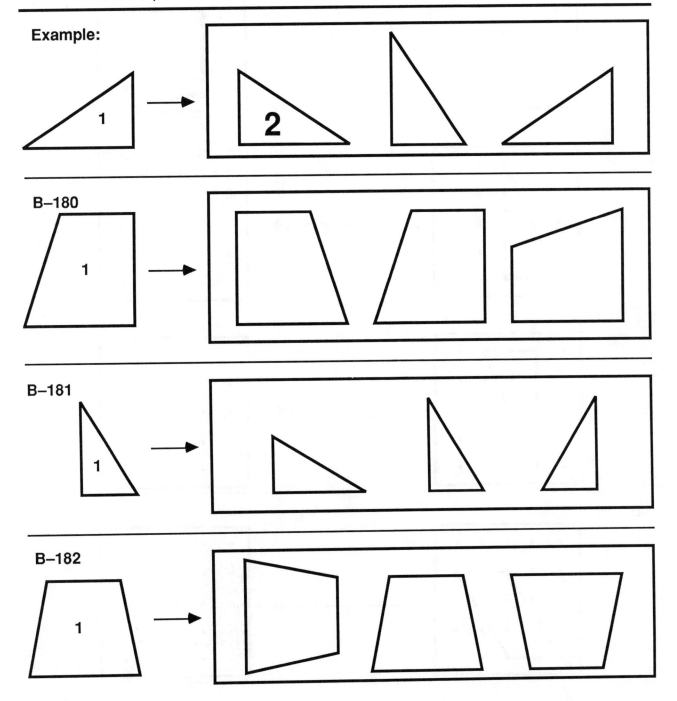

MOTIONS—FLIPS

A figure is pictured before a flip.
Draw the picture after the flip.

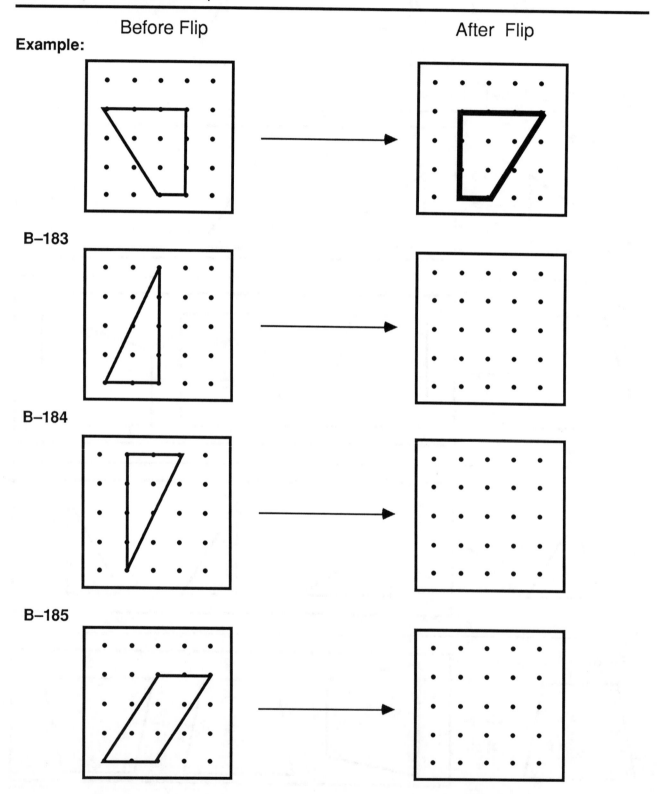

Before Flip   After Flip

Example:

B–183

B–184

B–185

MOTIONS—TURNS

If you turn triangle 1 you get triangle 2.

Write a 2 in the shape that shows a turn.

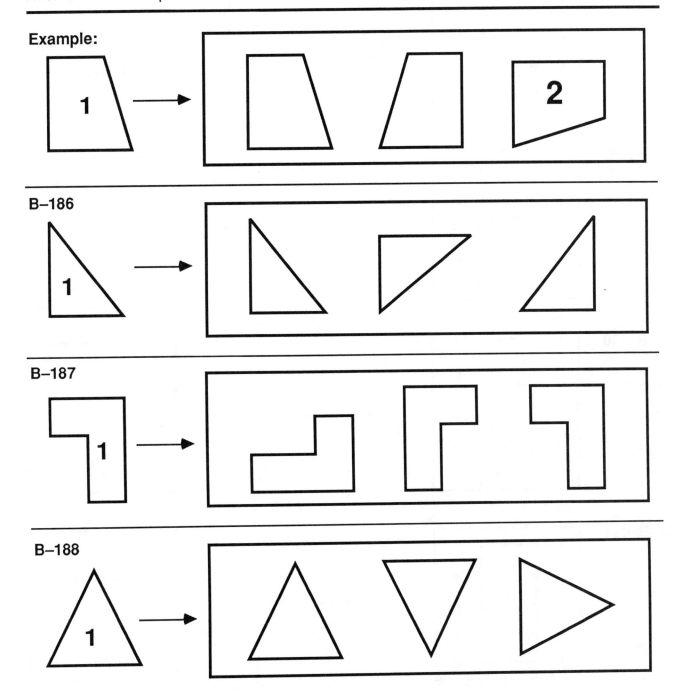

MOTIONS—TURNS

A figure is pictured before a turn.
Draw the picture after the turn.

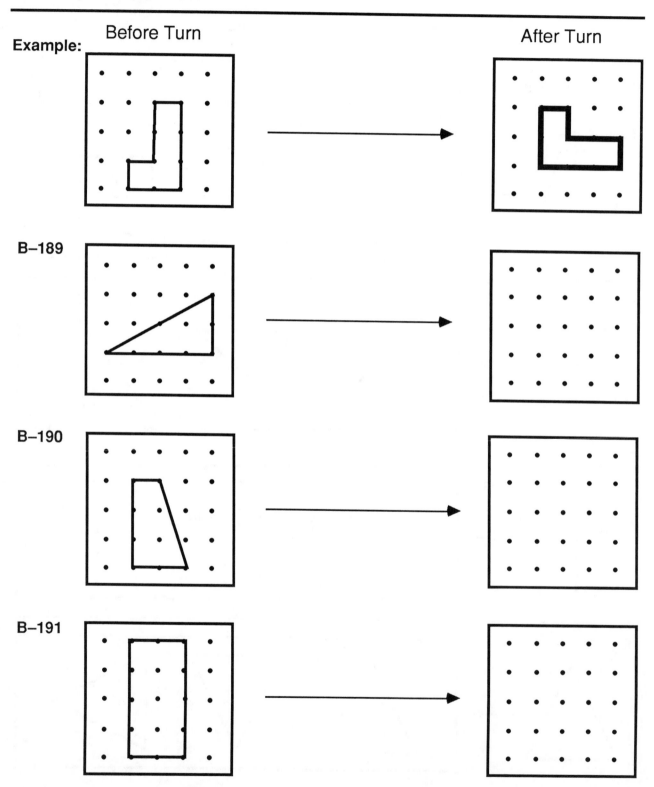

CONGRUENT FIGURES

Congruent figures are the same size and same shape.
Draw a line around the figure that is congruent to the figure in the box.

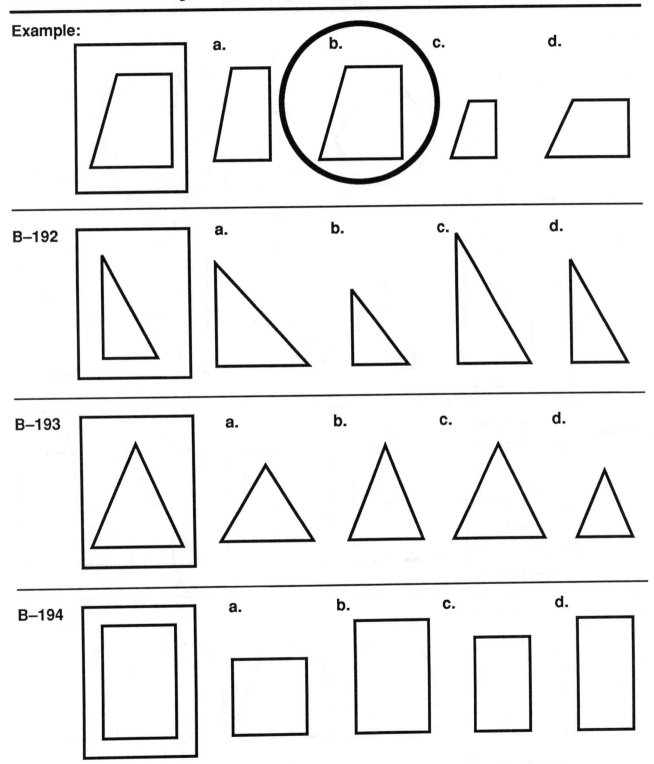

CONGRUENT FIGURES

Congruent figures are the same size and same shape.
Draw a line around the figure that is congruent to the figure in the box.

Example:

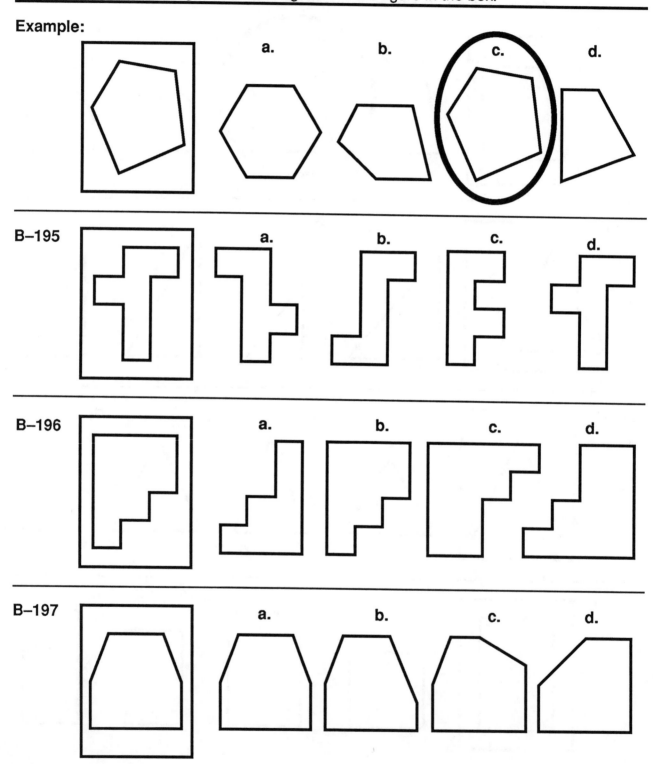

B–195

B–196

B–197

CONGRUENT FIGURES

Congruent figures are the same size and same shape.
Draw a line around the figures that are congruent to the shape in the box.
The matching figure has been flipped.

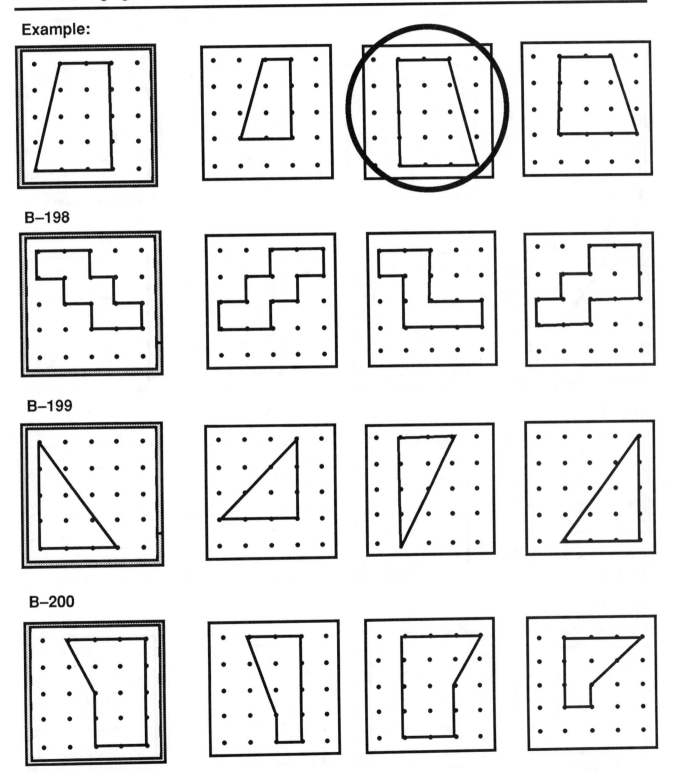

Example:

B–198

B–199

B–200

CONGRUENT FIGURES

Congruent figures are the same size and same shape.
Draw a line around the figures that are congruent to the shape in the box.
The matching figure has been turned.

Example:

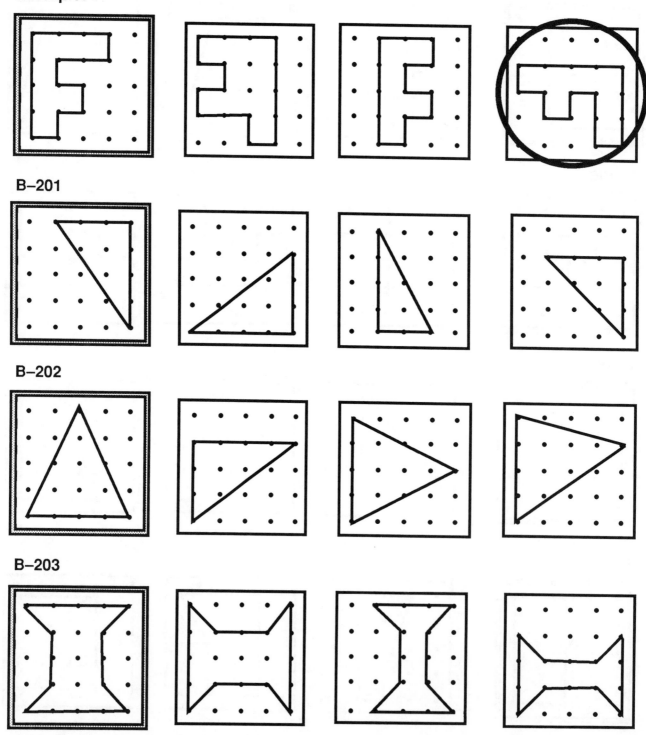

B–201

B–202

B–203

CONGRUENT FIGURES

Draw a congruent figure on the dot paper.

Example:

B–204

B–205

B–206

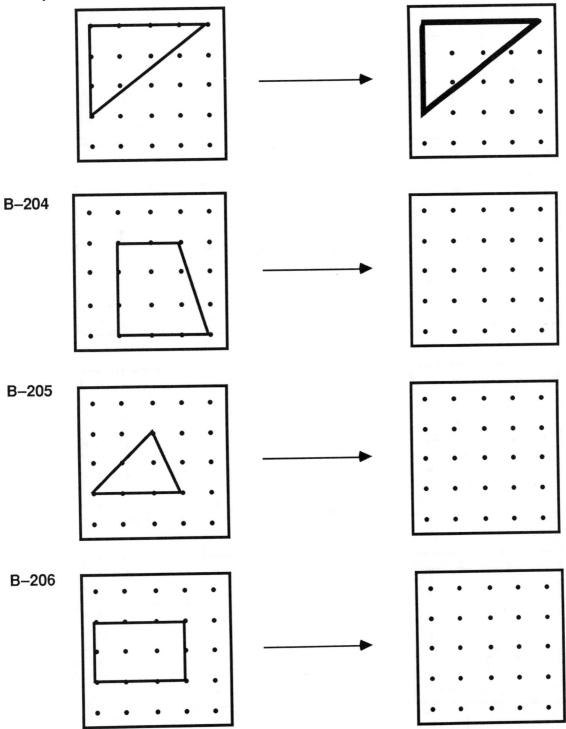

CONGRUENT FIGURES

Draw a congruent figure on the dot paper.

Example:

B–207

B–208

B–209

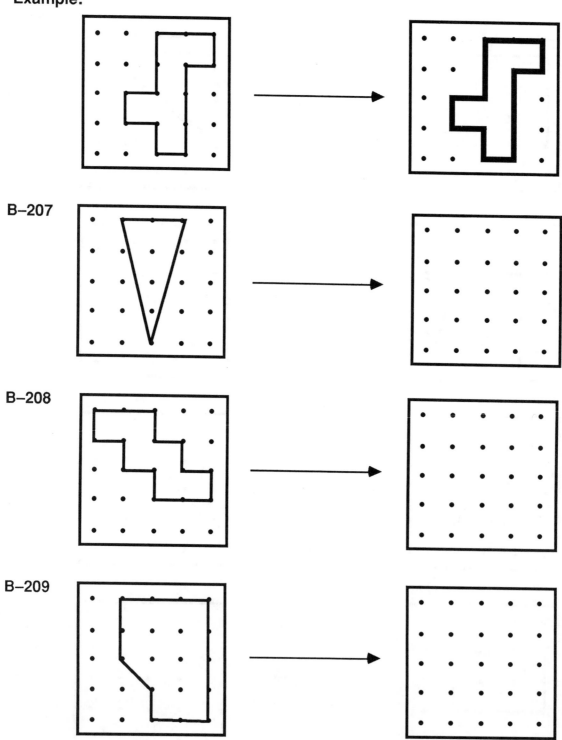

SIMILAR FIGURES

Similar figures have the same shape.
They are not always the same size.
Draw a line around the shape that is similar to the shaded shape.

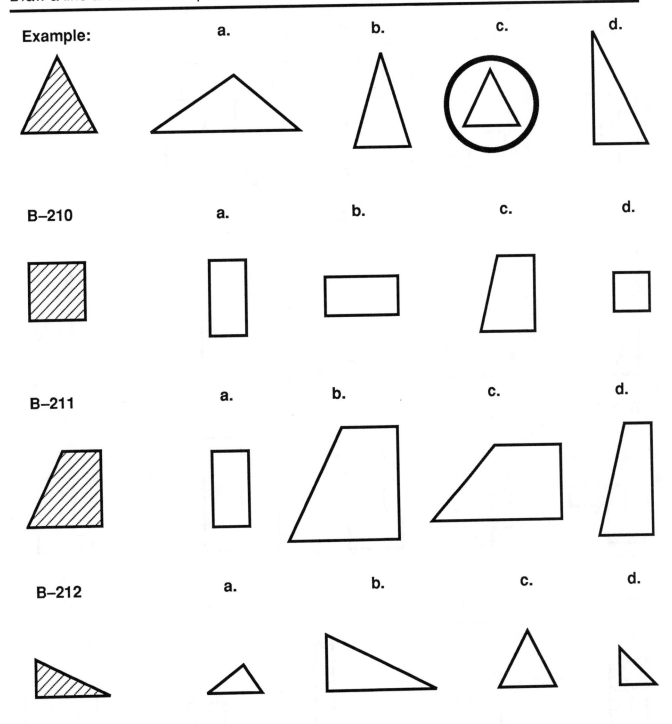

P.O. BOX 448, PACIFIC GROVE, CA 93950

SIMILAR FIGURES

Similar figures have the same shape.
They are not always the same size.
Draw a line around the shape that is similar to the shaded shape.

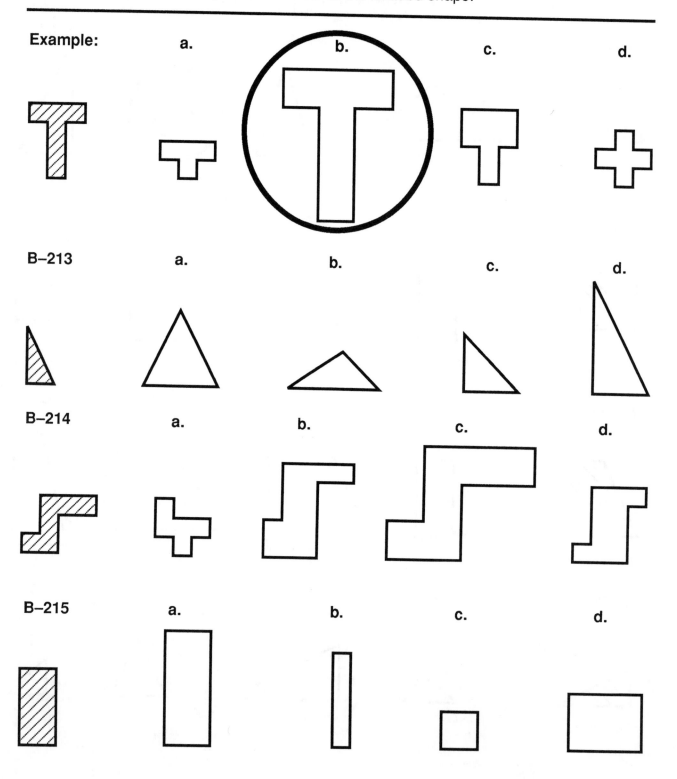

SIMILAR FIGURES

Similar figures have the same shape.
Draw a figure that is similar to the shaded figure.
Make it smaller than the shaded figure.

Example:

B–216

B–217

B–218

103   P.O. BOX 448, PACIFIC GROVE, CA 93950

SIMILAR FIGURES

Similar figures have the same shape.
Draw a figure that is similar to the shaded figure.
Make it larger than the shaded figure.

Example:

B–219

B–220

B–221

COMBINING SHAPES

Look at the two shaded shapes.

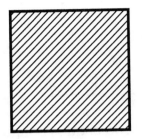

Put an X on all the figures that can be made by combining the two shaded shapes.

Example:

B–222

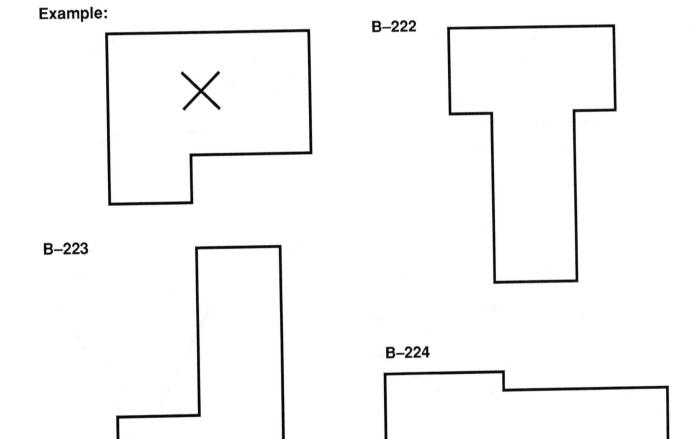

B–223

B–224

                          P.O. BOX 448, PACIFIC GROVE, CA 93950

COMBINING SHAPES

Look at the two shaded shapes.

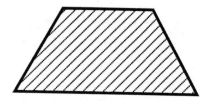 

Put an X on all the figures that can be made by combining the two shaded shapes.

Example:

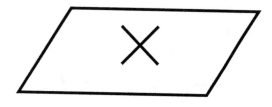

B–225

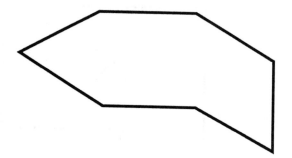

B–226

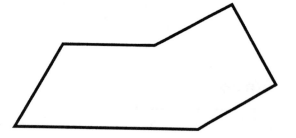

B–227

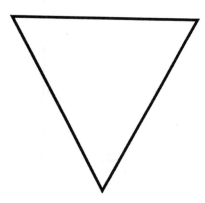

       P.O. BOX 448, PACIFIC GROVE, CA 93950

COMBINING SHAPES

Look at the two shaded shapes.

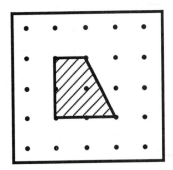

Put an X on all the shapes that can be made by combining the two shaded shapes.

Example:

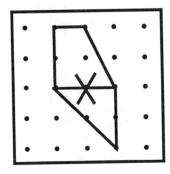

B–228

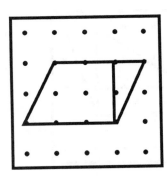

B–229

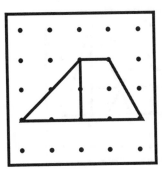

B–230

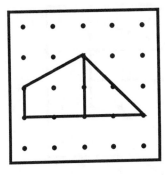

B–231

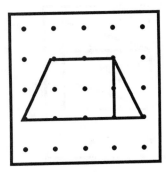

B–232

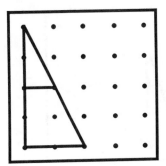

107   P.O. BOX 448, PACIFIC GROVE, CA 93950

COMBINING SHAPES

Look at the three shaded shapes.

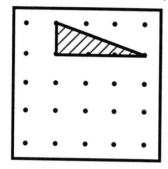 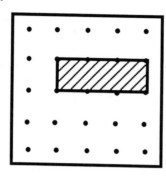 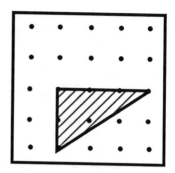

Put an ✕ on all the shapes that can be made by combining the three shaded shapes.

Example: **B–233**   **B–234**

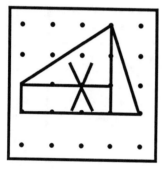 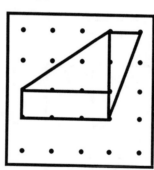 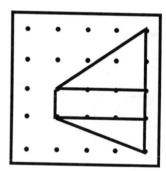

B–235   **B–236**   **B–237**

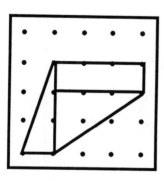 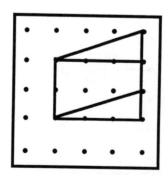 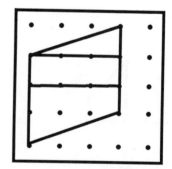

                                       P.O. BOX 448, PACIFIC GROVE, CA 93950

COMBINING SHAPES

Look at the two triangles below.

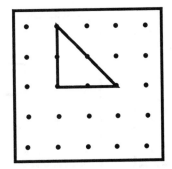 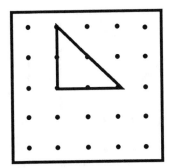

Combine the two triangles above to make a different figure in each box of dots below.

Example:

B–238

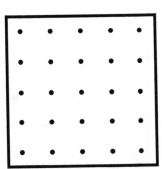

B–239

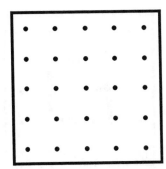

B–240

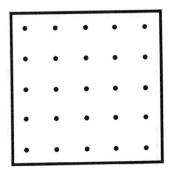

B–241

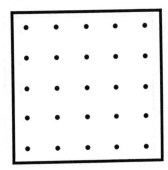

B–242

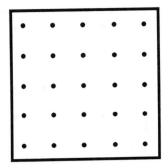

P.O. BOX 448, PACIFIC GROVE, CA 93950

COMBINING SHAPES

Look at the three shapes below.

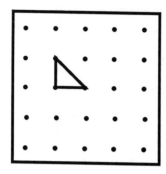 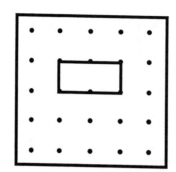 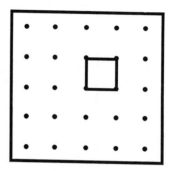

Combine the three shapes above to make a different figure in each box of dots below.

Example:

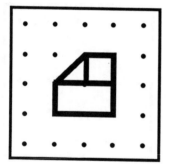

B-243

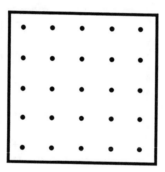

B-244

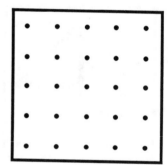

B-245

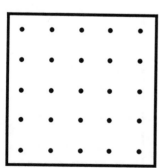

B-246

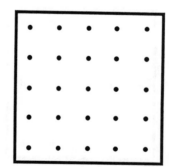

B-247

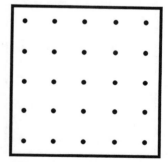

110   P.O. BOX 448, PACIFIC GROVE, CA 93950

MATCHING SHAPES

Match the figures that fit together to form a square.

Example:

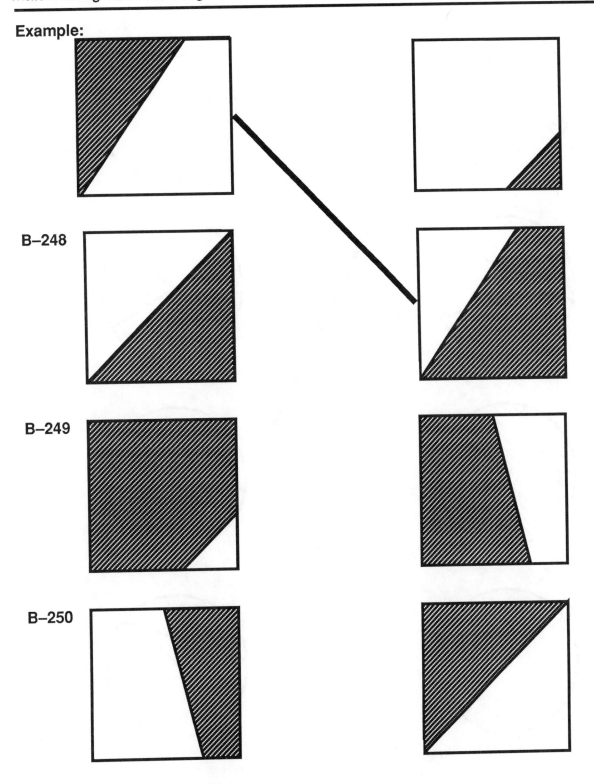

B–248

B–249

B–250

P.O. BOX 448, PACIFIC GROVE, CA 93950

MATCHING SHAPES

Match the figures that fit together to make a circle.

Example:

B–251

B–252

B–253

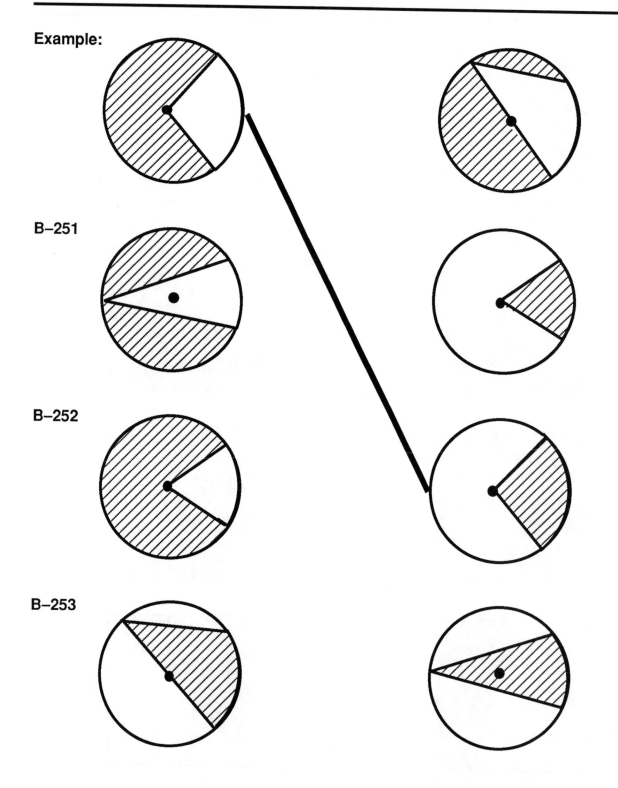

FINDING SHAPES

Put an ✕ on all the shapes you find in the figure.

Example:

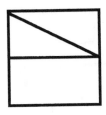

a.    b.

c.   d.

B–254

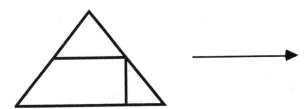

a. 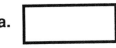   b.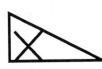

c.   d.

B–255

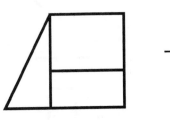

a.    b.

c.    d.

B–256

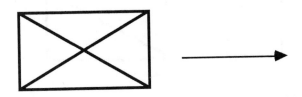

a.    b.

c. 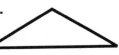   d.

       P.O. BOX 448, PACIFIC GROVE, CA 93950

FINDING SHAPES

Put an ✕ on all the shapes you find in the figure.

Example:

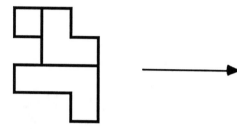

a.
b.

c.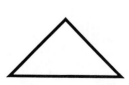
d.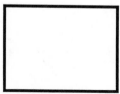

B–257

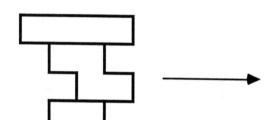

a.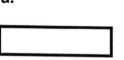
b.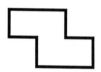

c.
d.

B–258

a.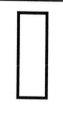
b.

c.
d.

B–259

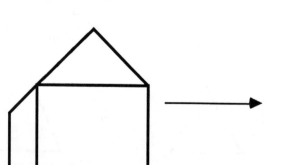

a.
b.

c.
d.

                                       P.O. BOX 448, PACIFIC GROVE, CA 93950

DIVIDING FIGURES

Connect dots to divide the figure into squares and triangles.

Example:

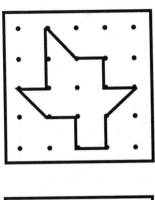

B–260

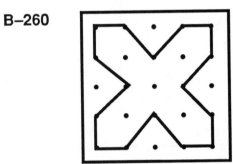

B–261

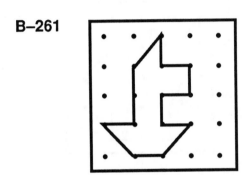

B–262

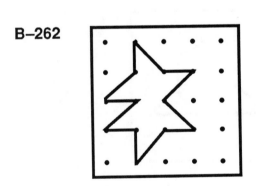

B–263

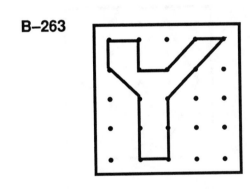

B–264

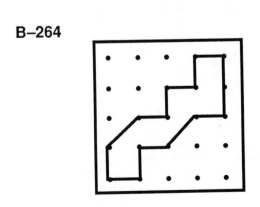

B–265

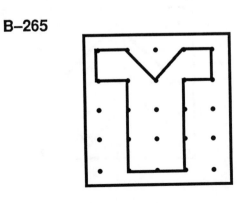

       P.O. BOX 448, PACIFIC GROVE, CA 93950

DIVIDING FIGURES

Connect dots to divide the figure into squares and triangles.

Example:

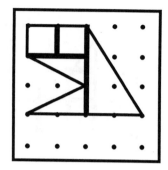

B–266

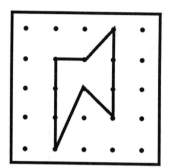

B–267

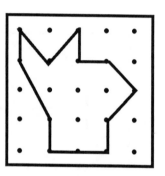

B–268

B–269

B–270

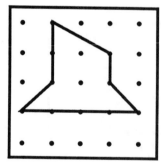

B–271

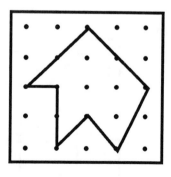

B–272

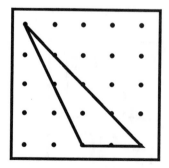

SETS OF FIVE

Match the sets that make a total of five dots.

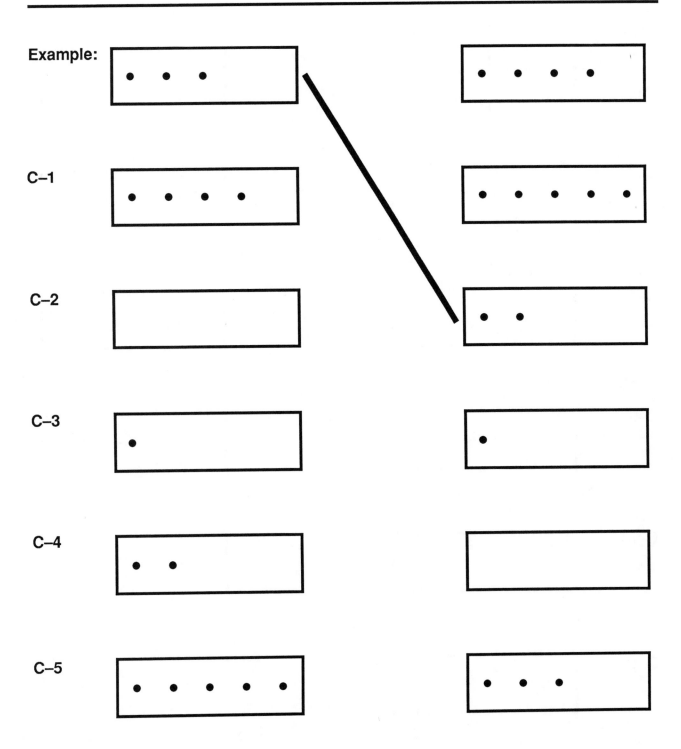

SETS OF SIX

Match the sets that make a total of six dots.

C–6

C–7

C–8

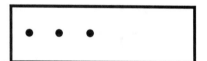

C–9

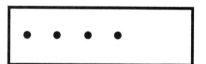

C–10

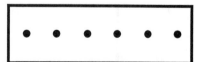

C–11

     118   P.O. BOX 448, PACIFIC GROVE, CA 93950

SETS OF NINE

Match the sets that make a total of nine dots.

C–12
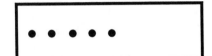

C–13

C–14

C–15
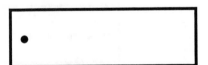

C–16
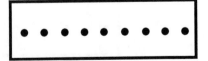

C–17

        119   P.O. BOX 448, PACIFIC GROVE, CA 93950

SETS OF TEN

Match the sets that make a total of ten dots.

C–18

C–19

C–20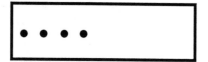

C–21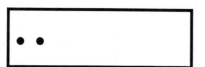

C–22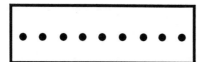

C–23

P.O. BOX 448, PACIFIC GROVE, CA 93950

NUMBER PATTERNS

Count the number of white squares in each row. Write the number in the chart.
Count the number of shaded squares in each row. Write the number in the chart.
Write the total number of squares in each row in the chart.

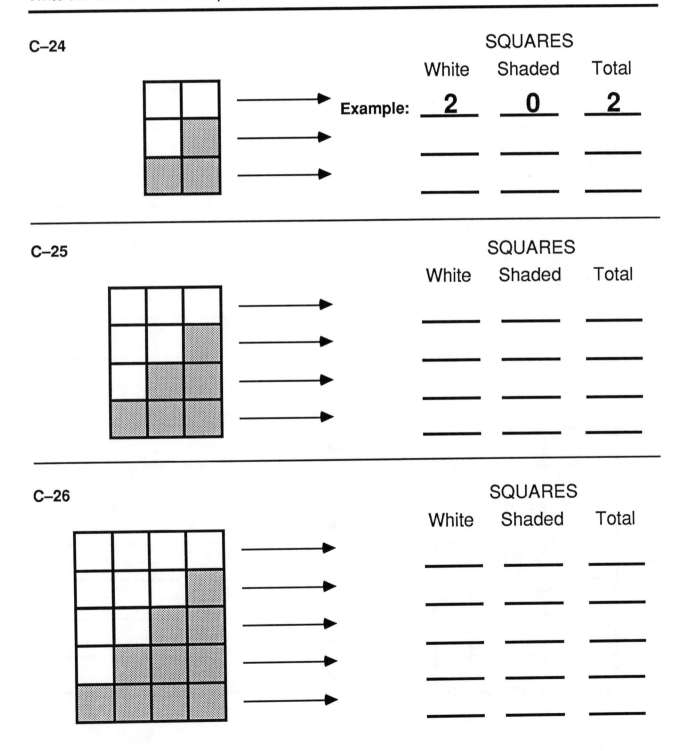

C–24

SQUARES

	White	Shaded	Total
Example:	2	0	2
	___	___	___
	___	___	___

C–25

SQUARES

White	Shaded	Total
___	___	___
___	___	___
___	___	___
___	___	___

C–26

SQUARES

White	Shaded	Total
___	___	___
___	___	___
___	___	___
___	___	___
___	___	___

                   P.O. BOX 448, PACIFIC GROVE, CA 93950

NUMBER PATTERNS

Count the number of white squares in each row. Write the number in the chart.
Count the number of shaded squares in each row. Write the number in the chart.
Write the total number of squares in each row in the chart.

C–27

	SQUARES		
	White	Shaded	Total
	___	___	___
	___	___	___
	___	___	___
	___	___	___
	___	___	___
	___	___	___
	___	___	___

C–28

	SQUARES		
	White	Shaded	Total
	___	___	___
	___	___	___
	___	___	___
	___	___	___
	___	___	___
	___	___	___
	___	___	___

P.O. BOX 448, PACIFIC GROVE, CA 93950

MAKING CHANGE

Which sets of coins are equal to one dime?
Circle the numbers of the sets.

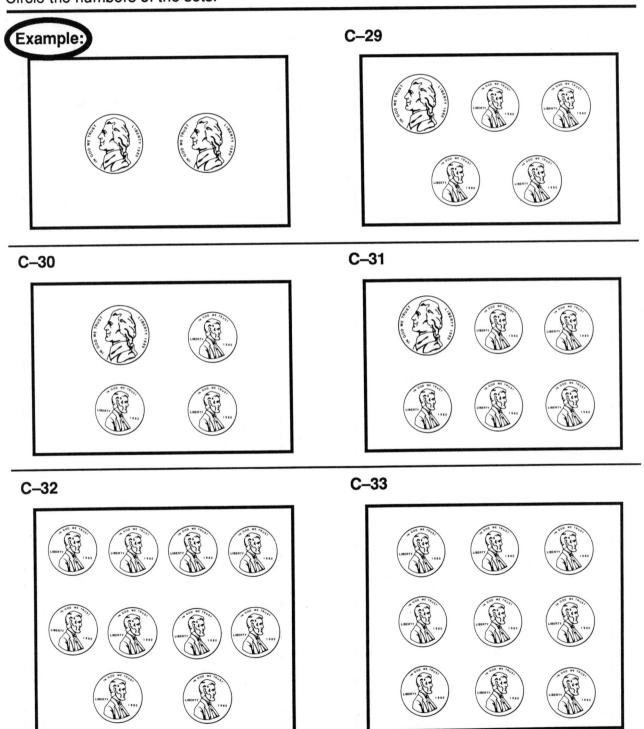

Example:

C–29

C–30

C–31

C–32

C–33

MAKING CHANGE

Which sets of coins are equal to one quarter?
Circle the numbers of the sets.

C–34

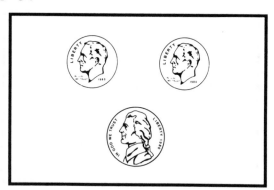

C–35

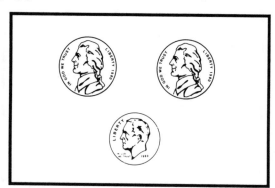

C–36

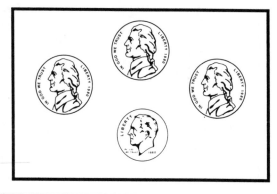

C–37

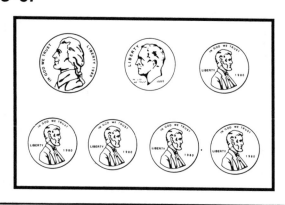

C–38

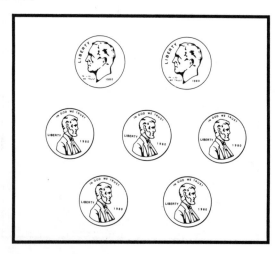

C–39

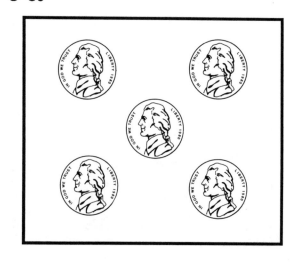

P.O. BOX 448, PACIFIC GROVE, CA 93950

MAKING SETS OF COINS

Put an X on the coins that are needed to make the number in the circle.

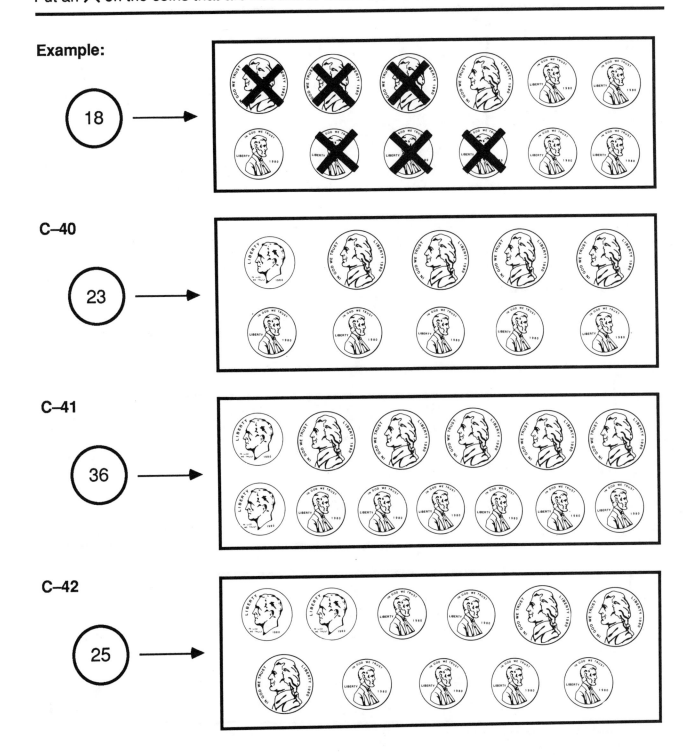

Example:

18

C–40

23

C–41

36

C–42

25

P.O. BOX 448, PACIFIC GROVE, CA 93950

MAKING SETS OF COINS

Put an X on the coins that are needed to make the number in the circle.

C–43

47 →

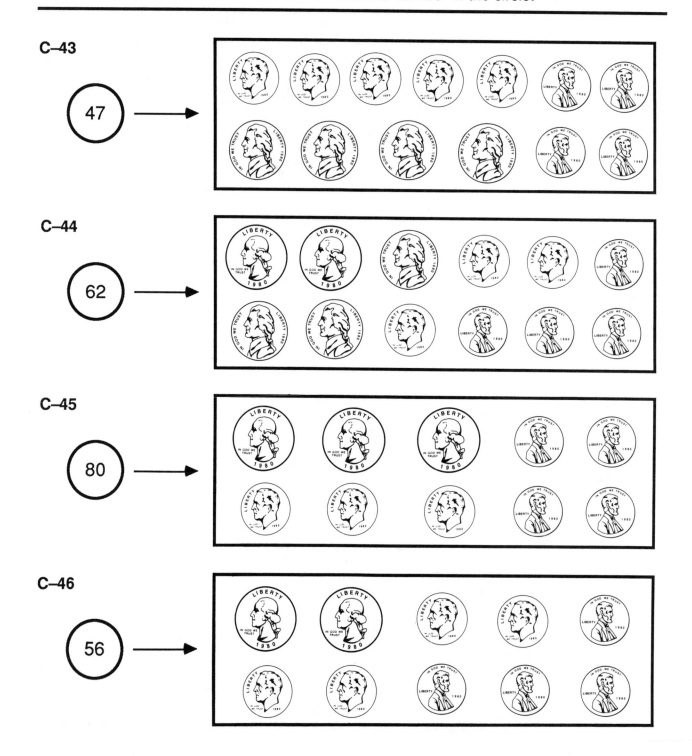

C–44

62 →

C–45

80 →

C–46

56 →

SUMS OF FIVE

Write the number of white circles in the first box.
Write the number of black circles in the second box.
Write the sum of the two numbers in the third box.

	White Circles		Black Circles		Sum

Example: ○ ○ ○ ○ ● | 4 + 1 = 5

C–47 ○ ○ ● ● ● | ☐ + ☐ = ☐

C–48 ○ ○ ○ ○ ○ | ☐ + ☐ = ☐

C–49 ○ ● ● ● ● | ☐ + ☐ = ☐

C–50 ○ ○ ○ ● ● | ☐ + ☐ = ☐

C–51 ● ● ● ● ● | ☐ + ☐ = ☐

P.O. BOX 448, PACIFIC GROVE, CA 93950

SUMS OF SIX

Write the number of white circles in the first box.
Write the number of black circles in the second box.
Write the sum of the two numbers in the third box.

	White Circles	Black Circles	Sum

C–52   ○ ○ ● ● ● ●   ☐ + ☐ = ☐

C–53   ○ ○ ○ ● ● ●   ☐ + ☐ = ☐

C–54   ○ ● ● ● ● ●   ☐ + ☐ = ☐

C–55   ○ ○ ○ ○ ● ●   ☐ + ☐ = ☐

C–56   ● ● ● ● ● ●   ☐ + ☐ = ☐

C–57   ○ ○ ○ ○ ○ ●   ☐ + ☐ = ☐

SUMS OF SIX AND SEVEN

Look at the number sentence.
Complete the sum.
Darken the correct number of circles for each sentence.

	White Circles		Black Circles		Sum	

Example: $2 + 4 = 6$ → ○○●●●●

C–58 $5 + 2 = $ → ○○○○○○○

C–59 $4 + 3 = $ → ○○○○○○○

C–60 $5 + 1 = $ → ○○○○○○

C–61 $0 + 7 = $ → ○○○○○○○

C–62 $3 + 3 = $ → ○○○○○○

SUMS OF NINE AND TEN

Look at the number sentence.
Complete the sum.
Darken the correct number of circles for each sentence.

	White Circles	Black Circles	Sum	

C–63 $6 + 3 = \square \longrightarrow$ OOOOOOOOO

C–64 $4 + 6 = \square \longrightarrow$ OOOOOOOOOO

C–65 $8 + 2 = \square \longrightarrow$ OOOOOOOOOO

C–66 $4 + 5 = \square \longrightarrow$ OOOOOOOOO

C–67 $7 + 3 = \square \longrightarrow$ OOOOOOOOOO

C–68 $2 + 7 = \square \longrightarrow$ OOOOOOOOO

P.O. BOX 448, PACIFIC GROVE, CA 93950

GROUPING BY TENS

Make groups of ten by filling in ten circles.
Write the number of tens and ones in the boxes

		Tens	Ones

Example:

1	3

C–69

C–70

C–71

C–72

C–73

P.O. BOX 448, PACIFIC GROVE, CA 93950

GROUPING BY TENS

Draw a line around groups of ten circles.
Write the number of tens and ones in the boxes.

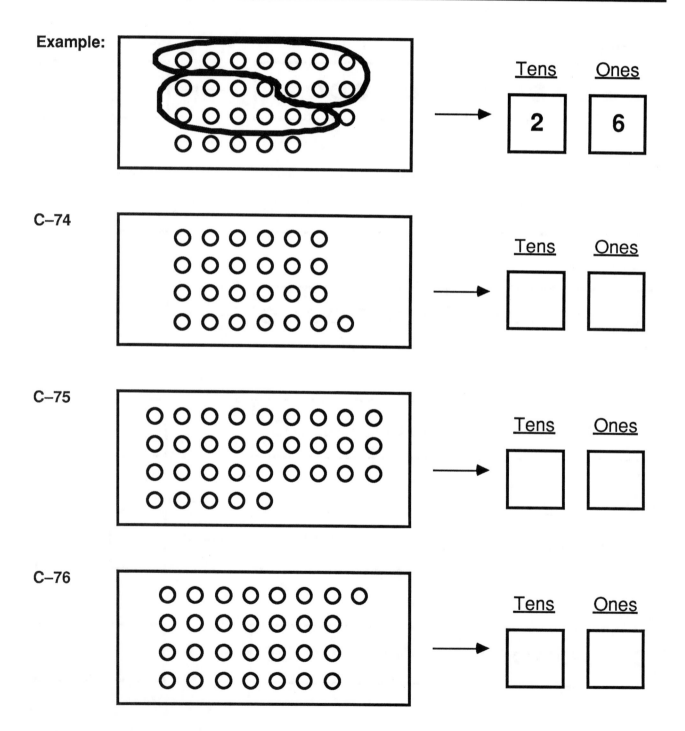

Example:

Tens | Ones
2 | 6

C–74

Tens | Ones

C–75

Tens | Ones

C–76

Tens | Ones

SUMS THAT ARE EQUAL

Circle all the problems in each row whose sums are equal to the first number in that row. There may be more than one correct answer.

Example:	14	6 + 7	(8 + 6)	4 + 9	(6 + 8)
C–77	9	5 + 5	3 + 6	6 + 4	4 + 4
C–78	16	8 + 8	9 + 8	6 + 9	7 + 9
C–79	11	1 + 9	9 + 2	5 + 6	8 + 4
C–80	12	9 + 2	8 + 4	3 + 8	4 + 9
C–81	8	7 + 2	6 + 1	2 + 6	7 + 1
C–82	18	6 + 9	9 + 9	8 + 9	7 + 9
C–83	15	9 + 6	9 + 7	6 + 9	8 + 8

P.O. BOX 448, PACIFIC GROVE, CA 93950

COMPARING SUMS

Find the sum of each addition problem below.
Write all the problems whose sums are less than 15 in the box on the left.
Write all the problems whose sums are more than 15 in the box on the right.

3 + 5	9 + 9	4 + 5	10 + 9
10 + 10	7 + 5	9 + 8	9 + 5
8 + 9	3 + 2	7 + 9	10 + 7
8 + 5	8 + 10	6 + 7	4 + 5

C–84 Less than 15 (<)

Example:
3 + 5

C–85 Greater than 15 (>)

C–86 Circle the problem with the largest sum in each box.

C–87 Place an X on the problem with the smallest sum in each box.

C–88 Which problem has the largest sum that is less than 15? _____

C–89 Which problem has the smallest sum that is more than 15? _____

COMPLETING SUMS OF TEN

Write a number in the box to make a sum of ten.

Example:

$$9$$
$$+ \boxed{1}$$
$$\overline{10}$$

C–90

$$2$$
$$+ \boxed{}$$
$$\overline{10}$$

C–91

$$\boxed{}$$
$$+ 3$$
$$\overline{10}$$

C–92

$$\boxed{}$$
$$+ 4$$
$$\overline{10}$$

C–93

$$5$$
$$+ \boxed{}$$
$$\overline{10}$$

C–94

$$6$$
$$+ \boxed{}$$
$$\overline{10}$$

C–95

$$\boxed{}$$
$$+ 7$$
$$\overline{10}$$

C–96

$$8$$
$$+ \boxed{}$$
$$\overline{10}$$

C–97

$$1$$
$$+ \boxed{}$$
$$\overline{10}$$

P.O. BOX 448, PACIFIC GROVE, CA 93950

COMPLETING SUMS OF TEN

Write a number in the box to make a sum of ten.

C–98

$$
\begin{array}{r}
2 \\
6 \\
+\ \boxed{} \\
\hline
10
\end{array}
$$

C–99

$$
\begin{array}{r}
3 \\
\boxed{} \\
+\ 7 \\
\hline
10
\end{array}
$$

C–100

$$
\begin{array}{r}
\boxed{} \\
1 \\
+\ 6 \\
\hline
10
\end{array}
$$

C–101

$$
\begin{array}{r}
\boxed{} \\
2 \\
+\ 1 \\
\hline
10
\end{array}
$$

C–102

$$
\begin{array}{r}
3 \\
\boxed{} \\
+\ 7 \\
\hline
10
\end{array}
$$

C–103

$$
\begin{array}{r}
6 \\
3 \\
+\ \boxed{} \\
\hline
10
\end{array}
$$

C–104

$$
\begin{array}{r}
2 \\
2 \\
+\ \boxed{} \\
\hline
10
\end{array}
$$

C–105

$$
\begin{array}{r}
2 \\
\boxed{} \\
+\ 4 \\
\hline
10
\end{array}
$$

C–106

$$
\begin{array}{r}
2 \\
0 \\
+\ \boxed{} \\
\hline
10
\end{array}
$$

P.O. BOX 448, PACIFIC GROVE, CA 93950

FINDING SUMS OF TEN

Circle two numbers that make a sum of ten.

Example:	5	(8)	6	3	(2)	1
C–107	4	5	7	8	9	5
C–108	3	4	5	7	8	3
C–109	1	8	9	3	4	5
C–110	9	5	3	4	2	6
C–111	7	2	6	3	5	9
C–112	4	2	5	7	1	8
C–113	8	5	4	3	6	1

P.O. BOX 448, PACIFIC GROVE, CA 93950

FINDING SUMS OF TEN

The first number is circled in each row.
Circle two more numbers so that the three numbers make a sum of ten.

Example:	(6)	5	(3)	6	(1)	8
C–114	(4)	8	5	1	7	4
C–115	(7)	4	2	5	1	8
C–116	(3)	4	6	3	5	9
C–117	(5)	6	4	1	5	7
C–118	(2)	3	2	4	6	5
C–119	(6)	4	2	3	2	5
C–120	(8)	1	3	2	4	1

MAKING LENGTHS EQUAL

Compare the lengths of A and B.
Draw a line around the number of squares that are needed to make A equal to B.

Example:

A

B

C–121

A

B

C–122

A

B

C–123

A

B

MAKING LENGTHS EQUAL

Compare the lengths of A and B.
Draw a line around the number of squares that are needed to make A equal to B.

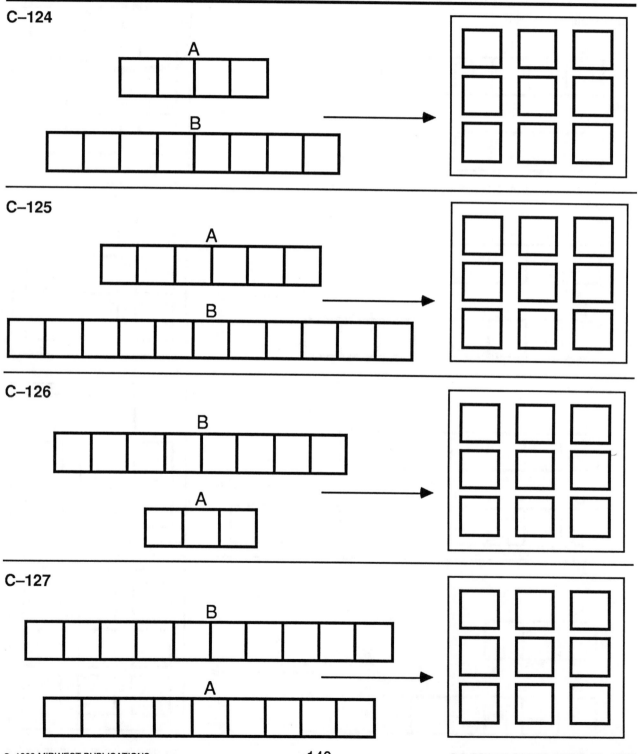

C–124

C–125

C–126

C–127

MAKING LENGTHS EQUAL

Compare the lengths of A and B.
Write the number of squares in B in the first box.
Write the number of squares in A in the second box.
Write the number of squares that are needed to make A equal to B in the third box.

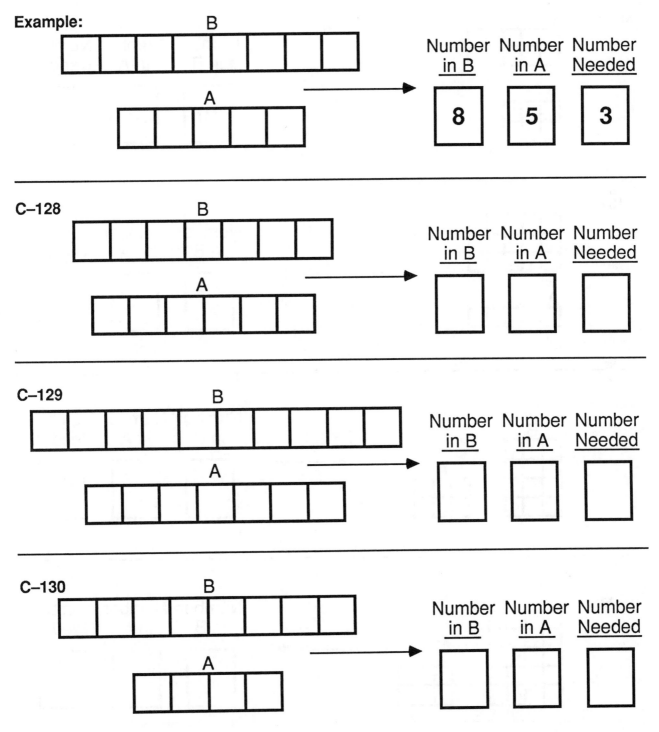

Example:

B

A

Number in B	Number in A	Number Needed
8	5	3

C–128

B

A

Number in B	Number in A	Number Needed

C–129

B

A

Number in B	Number in A	Number Needed

C–130

B

A

Number in B	Number in A	Number Needed

MAKING FIGURES EQUAL

Compare figures A and B.
Write the number of squares in figure B in the first box.
Write the number of squares in figure A in the second box.
Write the number of squares that are needed to make A equal to B in the third box.

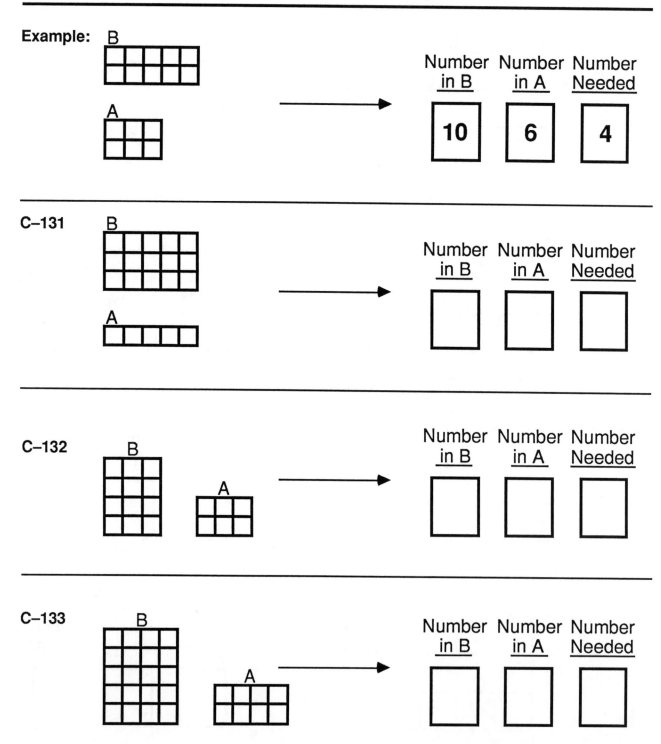

Example:

Number in B: **10**   Number in A: **6**   Number Needed: **4**

C–131

C–132

C–133

MISSING ADDENDS

Pick numbers from the set below to complete the sums.
You may need to use some numbers more than once.

```
8     15     4     12

13     5     11     7

6      3     9     14
```

Example:

7 + 8 = 15

C–134

☐ + 7 = 11

C–135

6 + ☐ = 14

C–136

8 + ☐ = 12

C–137

☐ + 7 = 12

C–138

☐ + ☐ = 15

C–139

☐ + ☐ = 13

C–140

☐ + ☐ = 11

MISSING ADDENDS

Write the correct number in the box.

Example:
$$9 + \boxed{7} = 16$$

C–141
$$\boxed{} + 7 = 13$$

C–142
$$\boxed{} + 4 = 9$$

C–143
$$\boxed{} + 8 = 11$$

C–144
$$9 + \boxed{} = 11$$

C–145
$$\boxed{} + 6 = 14$$

C–146
$$7 + \boxed{} = 11$$

C–147
$$5 + \boxed{} = 10$$

C–148
$$\boxed{} + 8 = 17$$

COMPLETING DIFFERENCES

Pick numbers from the set below to complete the differences.
You may need to use some numbers more than once.

4	8	11	6
10	7	15	13

Example:

$\boxed{11} - \boxed{7} = \boxed{4}$

C–149

$\boxed{} - \boxed{7} = \boxed{8}$

C–150

$\boxed{15} - \boxed{} = \boxed{7}$

C–151

$\boxed{} - \boxed{11} = \boxed{4}$

C–152

$\boxed{} - \boxed{6} = \boxed{7}$

C–153

$\boxed{10} - \boxed{} = \boxed{4}$

C–154

$\boxed{} - \boxed{} = \boxed{3}$

C–155

$\boxed{} - \boxed{} = \boxed{5}$

COMPLETING DIFFERENCES

Write the correct number in the box.

Example:
$$\begin{array}{r} 15 \\ -\;\boxed{8} \\ \hline 7 \end{array}$$

C–156
$$\begin{array}{r} 12 \\ -\;\boxed{} \\ \hline 5 \end{array}$$

C–157
$$\begin{array}{r} \boxed{} \\ -\;6 \\ \hline 4 \end{array}$$

C–158
$$\begin{array}{r} \boxed{} \\ -\;8 \\ \hline 9 \end{array}$$

C–159
$$\begin{array}{r} \boxed{} \\ -\;7 \\ \hline 3 \end{array}$$

C–160
$$\begin{array}{r} 18 \\ -\;\boxed{} \\ \hline 9 \end{array}$$

C–161
$$\begin{array}{r} \boxed{} \\ -\;8 \\ \hline 2 \end{array}$$

C–162
$$\begin{array}{r} 13 \\ -\;\boxed{} \\ \hline 8 \end{array}$$

C–163
$$\begin{array}{r} \boxed{} \\ -\;6 \\ \hline 10 \end{array}$$

 P.O. BOX 448, PACIFIC GROVE, CA 93950

DIFFERENCES THAT ARE EQUAL

Circle all the problems in each row whose differences equal the first number in that row.
There may be more than one correct answer.

Example:	6	 12 – 6	13 – 8	11 – 5	14 – 7
C–164	5	13 – 6	12 – 7	13 – 7	15 – 8
C–165	8	15 – 8	12 – 4	16 – 8	11 – 4
C–166	3	12 – 9	8 – 4	9 – 5	7 – 4
C–167	7	9 – 7	12 – 6	15 – 8	16 – 8
C–168	5	14 – 9	15 – 7	9 – 3	13 – 9
C–169	6	15 – 9	9 – 4	13 – 6	12 – 6
C–170	4	12 – 9	13 – 9	7 – 2	13 – 8

       P.O. BOX 448, PACIFIC GROVE, CA 93950

COMPARING DIFFERENCES

Find the difference of each subtraction problem below.
Write all the problems whose differences are less than 10 in the box on the left.
Write all the problems whose differences are more than 10 in the box on the right.

$15 - 7$	$18 - 6$	$13 - 7$	$16 - 9$
$16 - 3$	$17 - 6$	$14 - 9$	$15 - 3$
$18 - 9$	$16 - 2$	$18 - 4$	$14 - 7$
$17 - 3$	$13 - 5$	$17 - 2$	$12 - 5$

C–171 Less than 10 (<)

Example:

$15 - 7$

C–172 Greater than 10 (>)

C–173 Circle the problem with the largest difference in each box.

C–174 Place an $\times$ on the problem with the smallest difference in each box.

C–175 Which problem has the largest difference that is less than 10? _____

C–176 Which problem has the smallest difference that is more than 10? _____

EQUAL SETS

Match the sets that have the same amount of money.

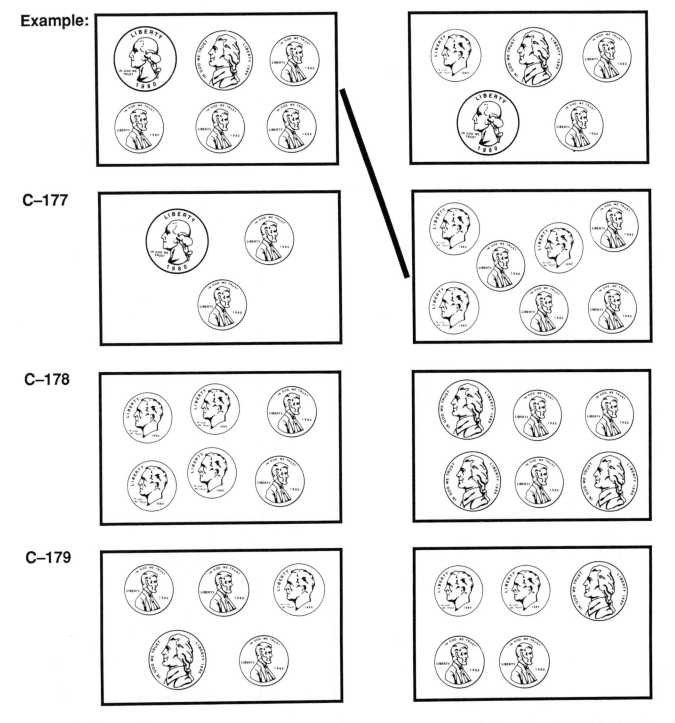

EQUAL SETS

Match the sets that have the same amount of money.

C–180

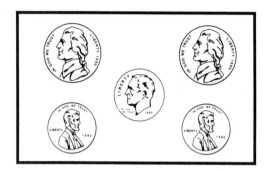

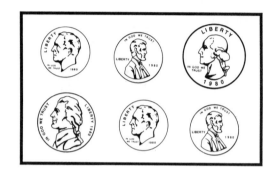

C–181

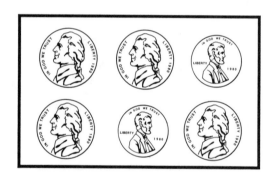

C–182

C–183

P.O. BOX 448, PACIFIC GROVE, CA 93950

EQUAL SETS

Circle the number that shows the amount of money in the set.

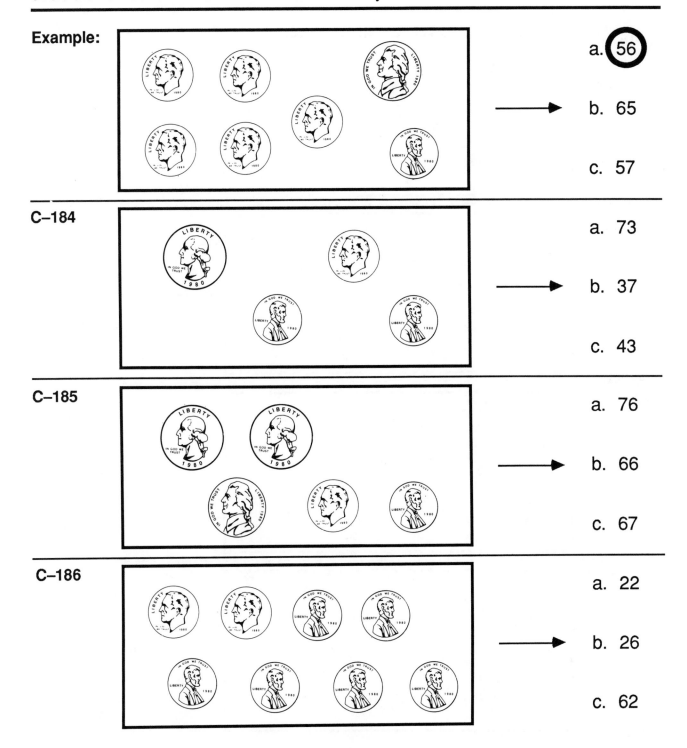

Example:

a. (56)

b. 65

c. 57

C–184

a. 73

b. 37

c. 43

C–185

a. 76

b. 66

c. 67

C–186

a. 22

b. 26

c. 62

EQUAL SETS

Circle the number that shows the amount of money in the set.

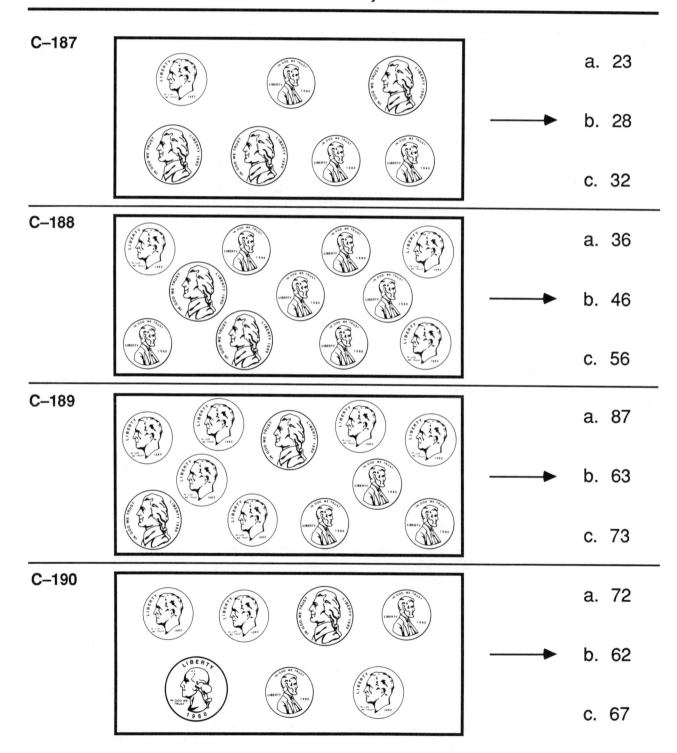

C–187

a. 23

→ b. 28

c. 32

C–188

a. 36

→ b. 46

c. 56

C–189

a. 87

→ b. 63

c. 73

C–190

a. 72

→ b. 62

c. 67

P.O. BOX 448, PACIFIC GROVE, CA 93950

COUNTING ARRAYS

Write the number of cubes in each row.
Write the total number of cubes in the circle.

Example: ▢ ▢ ▢ ▢ ⟶ __4__

▢ ▢ ▢ ▢ ⟶ __4__

⑧

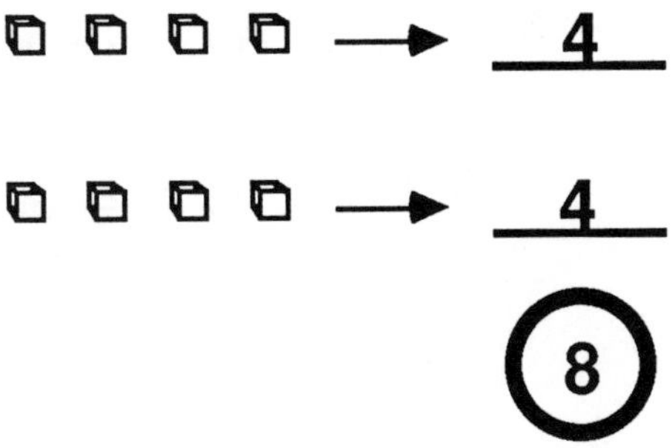

C–191 ▢ ▢ ▢ ▢ ⟶ _____

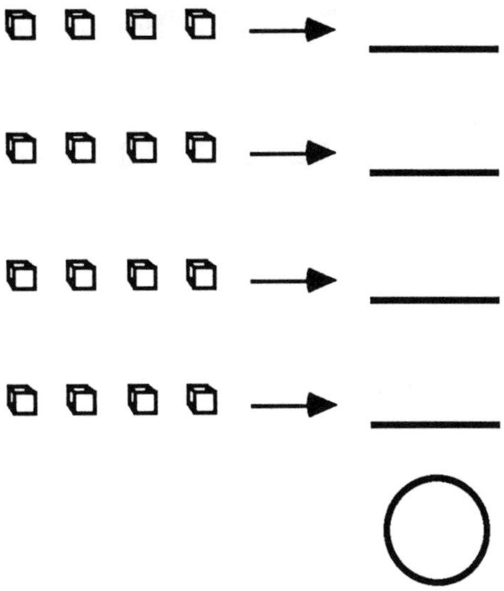

▢ ▢ ▢ ▢ ⟶ _____

▢ ▢ ▢ ▢ ⟶ _____

▢ ▢ ▢ ▢ ⟶ _____

◯

C–192 ▢ ▢ ▢ ▢ ⟶ _____

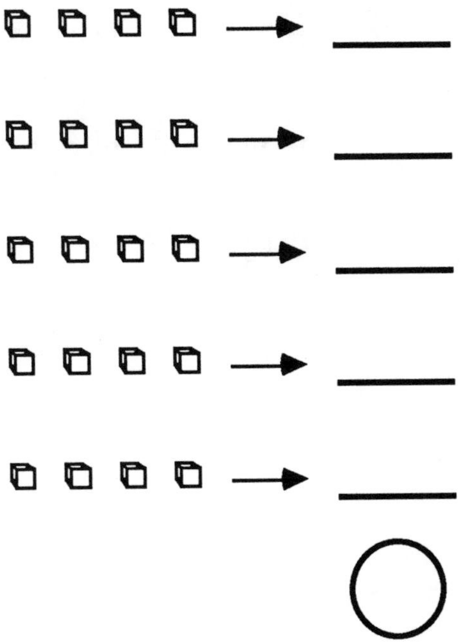

▢ ▢ ▢ ▢ ⟶ _____

▢ ▢ ▢ ▢ ⟶ _____

▢ ▢ ▢ ▢ ⟶ _____

▢ ▢ ▢ ▢ ⟶ _____

◯

C–193 ▢ ▢ ▢ ▢ ⟶ _____

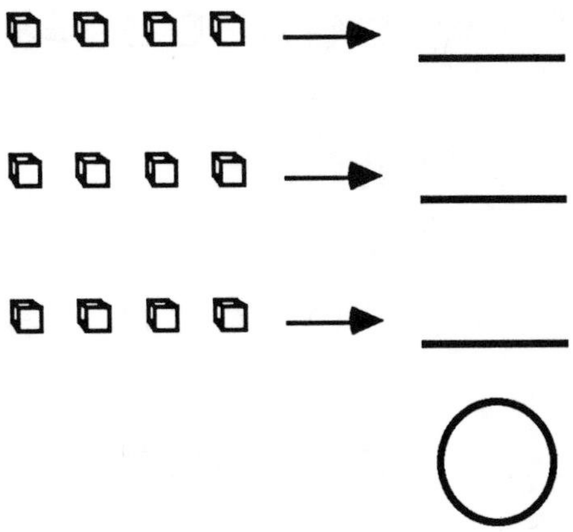

▢ ▢ ▢ ▢ ⟶ _____

▢ ▢ ▢ ▢ ⟶ _____

◯

COUNTING ARRAYS

Write the number of cubes in each row.
Write the total number of cubes in the circle.

C–194   🧊🧊🧊🧊🧊 ⟶ _____

🧊🧊🧊🧊🧊 ⟶ _____

◯

C–195   🧊🧊🧊🧊🧊 ⟶ _____

🧊🧊🧊🧊🧊 ⟶ _____

🧊🧊🧊🧊🧊 ⟶ _____

🧊🧊🧊🧊🧊 ⟶ _____

◯

C–196   🧊🧊🧊🧊🧊 ⟶ _____

🧊🧊🧊🧊🧊 ⟶ _____

🧊🧊🧊🧊🧊 ⟶ _____

🧊🧊🧊🧊🧊 ⟶ _____

🧊🧊🧊🧊🧊 ⟶ _____

◯

C–197   🧊🧊🧊🧊🧊 ⟶ _____

🧊🧊🧊🧊🧊 ⟶ _____

🧊🧊🧊🧊🧊 ⟶ _____

◯

© 1988 MIDWEST PUBLICATIONS   P.O. BOX 448, PACIFIC GROVE, CA 93950

COUNTING ARRAYS

For each set write the number of rows in the first box.
Write the number of cubes in each row in the second box.
Write the total number of cubes in the third box.

Example: C–198

   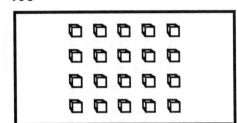

Rows   Cubes   Total Cubes   Rows   Cubes   Total Cubes

$$\boxed{3} \times \boxed{8} = \boxed{24}$$ $$\boxed{} \times \boxed{} = \boxed{}$$

C–199   C–200

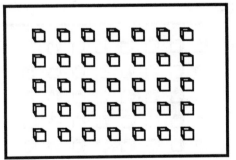   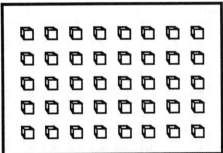

Rows   Cubes   Total Cubes   Rows   Cubes   Total Cubes

$$\boxed{} \times \boxed{} = \boxed{}$$ $$\boxed{} \times \boxed{} = \boxed{}$$

                                       P.O. BOX 448, PACIFIC GROVE, CA 93950

COUNTING ARRAYS

In each set write the number of rows in the first box.
Write the number of cubes in each row in the second box.
Write the total number of cubes in the third box.

C–201

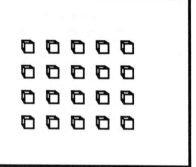

Rows　　　Cubes　　　Total Cubes

☐ × ☐ = ☐

C–202

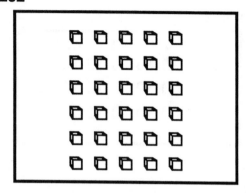

Rows　　　Cubes　　　Total Cubes

☐ × ☐ = ☐

C–203

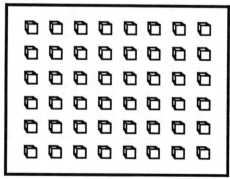

Rows　　　Cubes　　　Total Cubes

☐ × ☐ = ☐

C–204

Rows　　　Cubes　　　Total Cubes

☐ × ☐ = ☐

　　　　　　　　　　P.O. BOX 448, PACIFIC GROVE, CA 93950

PRODUCTS THAT ARE EQUAL

Circle all the problems in each row whose products equal the first number in that row. There may be more than one correct answer.

Example:	48	7×7	$\boxed{6 \times 8}$	8×7	5×8
C–205	12	4×3	2×5	4×4	2×6
C–206	45	8×5	7×7	5×9	6×8
C–207	36	4×8	9×4	5×6	6×6
C–208	16	8×2	3×4	4×4	5×3
C–209	30	4×8	7×4	5×6	6×6
C–210	18	6×3	2×9	4×4	3×7
C–211	24	4×5	6×4	3×8	5×5

COMPARING PRODUCTS

Find the product of each multiplication problem below.
Write all the problems whose products are less than 40 in the box on the left.
Write all the problems whose products are more than 40 in the box on the right.

2×8	6×3	7×7	9×3
7×8	8×9	4×8	6×7
3×5	8×8	9×9	5×5
7×9	4×4	4×9	6×9

C–212   Less than 40 (<)

Example:

2×8

C–213   Greater than 40 (>)

C–214 Circle the problem with the largest product in each box.

C–215 Place an ✕ on the problem with the smallest product in each box.

C–216 Which problem has the largest product that is less than 40? _____

C–217 Which problem has the smallest product that is more than 40? _____

MISSING FACTORS

Write the correct number in the box.

Example:

$$\begin{array}{r} \boxed{8} \\ \times\ \underline{5} \\ 40 \end{array}$$

C–218

$$\begin{array}{r} \boxed{} \\ \times\ \underline{8} \\ 40 \end{array}$$

C–219

$$\begin{array}{r} \boxed{} \\ \times\ \underline{3} \\ 27 \end{array}$$

C–220

$$\begin{array}{r} 6 \\ \boxed{} \\ \times\ \underline{} \\ 24 \end{array}$$

C–221

$$\begin{array}{r} \boxed{} \\ \times\ \underline{9} \\ 81 \end{array}$$

C–222

$$\begin{array}{r} 4 \\ \boxed{} \\ \times\ \underline{} \\ 28 \end{array}$$

C–223 $2 \times \boxed{} = 6$

C–224 $\boxed{} \times 7 = 42$

C–225 $7 \times \boxed{} = 49$

C–226 $\boxed{} \times 6 = 48$

P.O. BOX 448, PACIFIC GROVE, CA 93950

MISSING FACTORS

Write the correct numbers in the boxes.

C–227

$40 = 5 \times \boxed{}$

C–228

$50 = 5 \times \boxed{}$

C–229

$15 = \boxed{} \times 3$

C–230

$9 \times \boxed{} = 63$

C–231

$8 = \boxed{} \times 8$

C–232

$7 = 7 \times \boxed{}$

C–233

$12 = 3 \times \boxed{}$

C–234

$12 = 3 \times \boxed{} \times \boxed{}$

C–235

$18 = 2 \times \boxed{}$

C–236

$18 = 2 \times \boxed{} \times \boxed{}$

P.O. BOX 448, PACIFIC GROVE, CA 93950

USING OPERATIONS

Choose two different numbers from the set below that will give you...

2	6	7	5
8	3	9	4

Example: the largest sum.

$$\boxed{9} + \boxed{8} = \boxed{17}$$

C–237   the smallest sum.

$$\boxed{} + \boxed{} = \boxed{}$$

C–238   the largest difference.

$$\boxed{} - \boxed{} = \boxed{}$$

C–239   the smallest difference.

$$\boxed{} - \boxed{} = \boxed{}$$

C–240   the largest product.

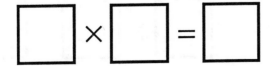

C–241   the smallest product.

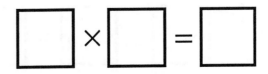

161   P.O. BOX 448, PACIFIC GROVE, CA 93950

USING OPERATIONS

Choose two different numbers from the set below that will give you...

2	4	7	5
6	8	10	3

C–242   the largest sum.

☐ + ☐ = ☐

C–243   the smallest sum.

☐ + ☐ = ☐

C–244   the largest difference.

☐ – ☐ = ☐

C–245   the smallest difference.

☐ – ☐ = ☐

C–246   the largest product.

☐ × ☐ = ☐

C–247   the smallest product.

☐ × ☐ = ☐

WHICH OPERATION DO YOU USE?

Circle the calculation that solves each problem.

Example:

The coach has 9 cans of tennis balls.
Each can holds 3 tennis balls.
How many tennis balls does the coach have?

9 + 3	9 − 3
(9 × 3)	9 ÷ 3

C–248

There are 18 people in class but only 9 chairs.
The teacher sends for enough chairs so that
everyone can be seated.
How many chairs do they need?

18 + 9	18 − 9
18 × 9	18 ÷ 9

C–249

There are 12 eggs in a carton.
You use 4 to make scrambled eggs.
How many are left in the carton?

12 + 4	12 − 4
12 × 4	12 ÷ 4

C–250

Four quarters equals one dollar.
John has 20 quarters.
How many dollars does John have?

20 + 4	20 − 4
20 × 4	20 ÷ 4

C–251

Eric has 6 dollars.
He earns 3 more dollars.
How many dollars does he have?

6 + 3	6 − 3
6 × 3	6 ÷ 3

                                       P.O. BOX 448, PACIFIC GROVE, CA 93950

WHICH OPERATION DO YOU USE?

Circle the calculation that solves each problem.

C–252

A family drove 2 miles to town.
On the way back they took a longer
route which was 4 miles.
How many miles more was the longer route?

4 + 2	4 – 2
4 × 2	4 ÷ 2

C–253

Our team played in two play-off games.
We scored 12 points in the first game and
6 points in the second game.
What was the total number of points we scored?

12 + 6	12 – 6
12 × 6	12 ÷ 6

C–254

A penny roll holds 50 pennies.
Tim has 3 penny rolls.
How many pennies does Tim have?

50 + 3	50 – 3
50 × 3	50 ÷ 3

C–255

A large pizza is cut into 12 pieces.
Ann wants to divide it evenly among
herself and 3 friends.
How many pieces should each person get?

12 + 3	12 – 3
12 + 4	12 – 4
12 × 3	12 ÷ 3
12 × 4	12 ÷ 4

C–256

Amy and 4 of her friends sold raffle tickets.
Each sold 10 tickets.
How many did they sell all together?

4 + 10	10 – 4
5 + 10	10 – 5
4 × 10	10 ÷ 4
5 × 10	10 ÷ 5

ROUNDING TO 10

Circle the number nearest in size to the number in the box.

Example:	8	⟶	(10)	40	30	20
C–257	12	⟶	30	20	40	10
C–258	18	⟶	20	30	10	0
C–259	24	⟶	10	20	40	30
C–260	48	⟶	30	40	50	60
C–261	76	⟶	70	60	80	50
C–262	14	⟶	10	30	20	40
C–263	34	⟶	40	20	30	50

165   P.O. BOX 448, PACIFIC GROVE, CA 93950

ROUNDING TO 10 AND 100

Round each number in the top set to the nearest 10.
Round each number in the bottom set to the nearest 100.

Example:

28 ⟶ **30**

C–264

14 ⟶ ☐

C–265

59 ⟶ ☐

C–266

47 ⟶ ☐

C–267

18 ⟶ ☐

C–268

88 ⟶ ☐

Example:

296 ⟶ **300**

C–269

112 ⟶ ☐

C–270

419 ⟶ ☐

C–271

688 ⟶ ☐

C–272

372 ⟶ ☐

C–273

590 ⟶ ☐

P.O. BOX 448, PACIFIC GROVE, CA 93950

ROUNDING

Look at the numbers in the box.
Put all the numbers closer to 40 than 50 in the box on the left.
Put all the numbers closer to 50 than 40 in the box on the right.

41	52	46	40
53	39	43	50
37	47	51	48
42	49	38	44

C–274 Closer to 40

Example:

41

C–275 Closer to 50

© 1988 MIDWEST PUBLICATIONS

P.O. BOX 448, PACIFIC GROVE, CA 93950

ROUNDING

Look at the addition problems in the box.
Put all the problems whose sums are closer to 10 than 20 in the box on the left.
Put all the problems whose sums are closer to 20 than 10 in the box on the right.

3 + 6	4 + 9	10 + 7	9 + 5	11 + 10
6 + 8	8 + 9	8 + 2	7 + 9	5 + 7
6 + 10	7 + 4	9 + 10	6 + 6	9 + 2
7 + 7	8 + 8	6 + 7	9 + 9	5 + 8

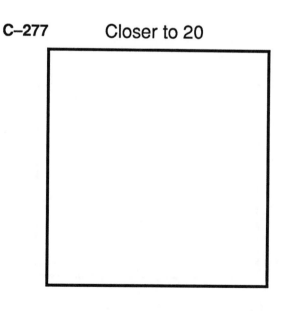

C–276   Closer to 10

Example:

3 + 6

C–277   Closer to 20

MULTIPLYING BY 10 AND 100

Write the answers in the boxes.

Example:

$5 \times 3 =$ | **15**

$5 \times 30 =$ | **150**

C–278

$2 \times 8 =$

$20 \times 8 =$

C–279

$9 \times 4 =$

$9 \times 40 =$

C–280

$6 \times 5 =$

$6 \times 50 =$

C–281

$4 \times 2 =$

$4 \times 200 =$

C–282

$4 \times 7 =$

$400 \times 7 =$

C–283

$3 \times 300 =$

C–284

$8 \times 90 =$

C–285

$700 \times 5 =$

C–286

$6 \times 800 =$

P.O. BOX 448, PACIFIC GROVE, CA 93950

ESTIMATING PRODUCTS

Round the underlined number to the nearest 10.
Write the answer in the circle.
Multiply the rounded answer by the number in the dotted box.
Write the product in the box.

Example:

Rounded

Product

$\underline{19} \times \boxed{5} \longrightarrow \bigcirc 20 \times 5 = \boxed{100}$

C–287

Rounded

Product

$\boxed{6} \times \underline{48} \longrightarrow 6 \times \bigcirc = \boxed{}$

C–288

Rounded

Product

$\boxed{8} \times \underline{72} \longrightarrow 8 \times \bigcirc = \boxed{}$

C–289

Rounded

Product

$\underline{37} \times \boxed{7} \longrightarrow \bigcirc \times 7 = \boxed{}$

C–290

Rounded

Product

$\boxed{9} \times \underline{21} \longrightarrow 9 \times \bigcirc = \boxed{}$

C–291

Rounded

Product

$\underline{59} \times \boxed{4} \longrightarrow \bigcirc \times 4 = \boxed{}$

P.O. BOX 448, PACIFIC GROVE, CA 93950

COMPARING LENGTHS

Squares are joined together to make two rods.
Circle the number that tells how many squares must be added to make the two equal.

Example:

a. 6
b. 3
c. 5

D–1

a. 4
b. 3
c. 6

D–2

a. 6
b. 3
c. 2

D–3

a. 4
b. 3
c. 5

D–4

a. 2
b. 5
c. 7

D–5

a. 4
b. 2
c. 3

D–6

a. 3
b. 9
c. 4

D–7

a. 2
b. 3
c. 1

COMPARING LENGTHS

Squares are joined together to make a rod.
Circle the number that tells how many squares must be added to make a length of 10.

Example:

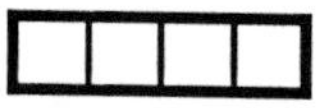

a. 8

b. 4

c. 6 (circled)

D–8

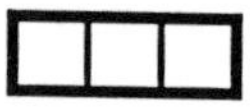

a. 7

b. 6

c. 3

D–9

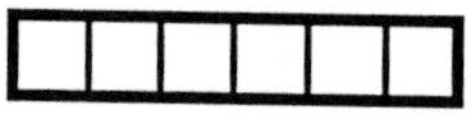

a. 6

b. 8

c. 4

D–10

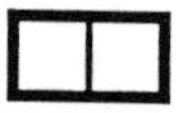

a. 4

b. 8

c. 2

D–11

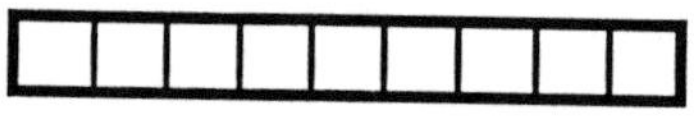

a. 2

b. 0

c. 1

D–12

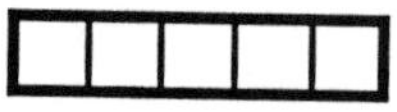

a. 5

b. 4

c. 6

D–13

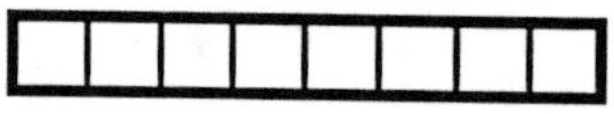

a. 1

b. 2

c. 4

D–14

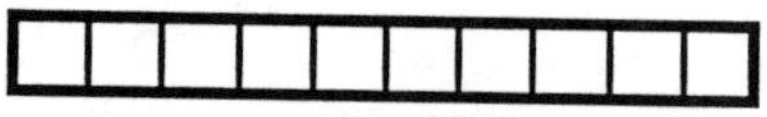

a. 1

b. 3

c. 0

FINDING LENGTHS OF PATHS

Squares are joined together to make a path.
Count the squares to find the length of the path from A to B.
Write the answer in the box.

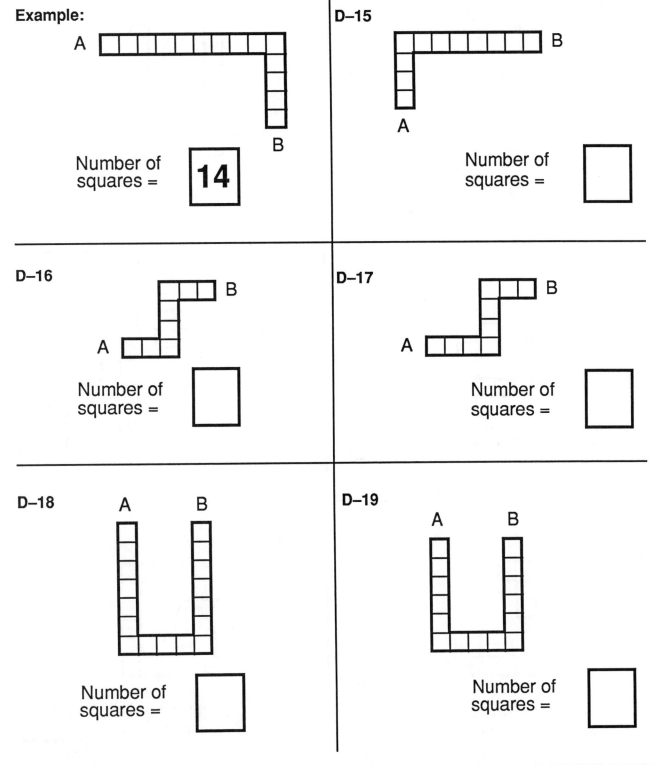

Example:

A

B

Number of
squares =   **14**

D–15

B

A

Number of
squares =

D–16

B

A

Number of
squares =

D–17

B

A

Number of
squares =

D–18

A   B

Number of
squares =

D–19

A   B

Number of
squares =

                                                   P.O. BOX 448, PACIFIC GROVE, CA 93950

FINDING LENGTHS OF PATHS

Squares are joined together to make a path.
Count the squares to find the length of the path from A to B.
Write the answer in the box.

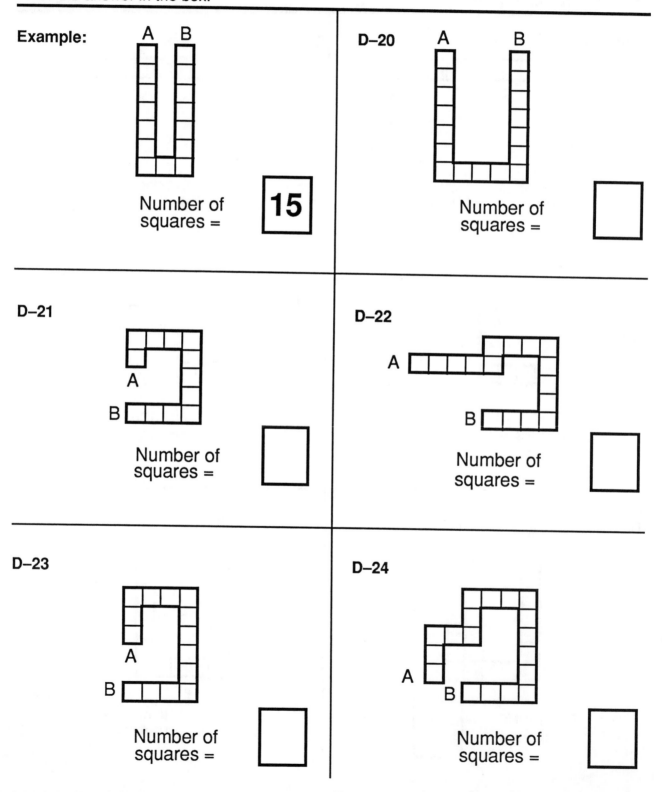

Example:

Number of squares = **15**

D–20

Number of squares =

D–21

Number of squares =

D–22

Number of squares =

D–23

Number of squares =

D–24

Number of squares =

174   P.O. BOX 448, PACIFIC GROVE, CA 93950

FINDING LENGTHS OF PATHS

Find the length of the path from A to B.
Write the answer in the box.
Put an ✕ on all the paths that are the same length as the path in the example.

Example:

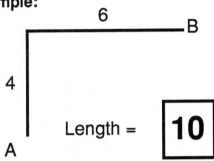

Length = **10**

D–25

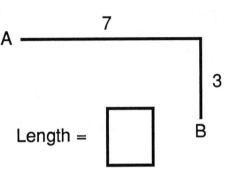

Length = ☐

D–26

Length = ☐

D–27

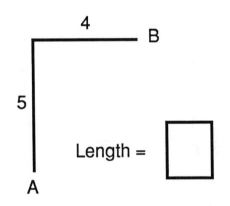

Length = ☐

D–28

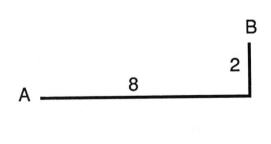

Length = ☐

D–29

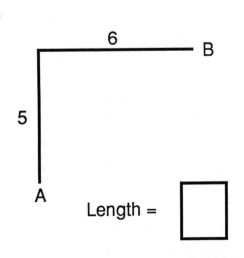

Length = ☐

FINDING LENGTHS OF PATHS

Find the length of the path from A to B.
Write the answer in the box.
Put an ✕ on all the paths that are the same length as the path in the example.

Example:

5

B

3

A

Length = **8**

D–30

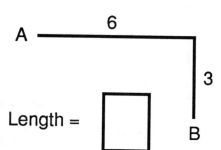

Length =

D–31

4

B

4

A

Length =

D–32

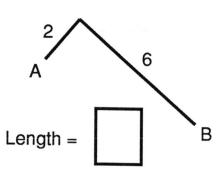

Length =

D–33

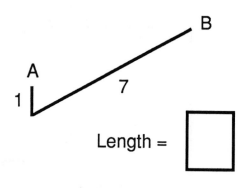

Length =

D–34

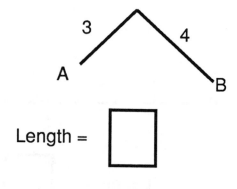

Length =

                                         P.O. BOX 448, PACIFIC GROVE, CA 93950

FINDING LENGTHS OF PATHS

Find the length of each path. Write the answer in the box.
Draw a line between boxes that contain paths that are the same length.

Example:

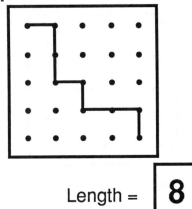

Length = **8**

D–35

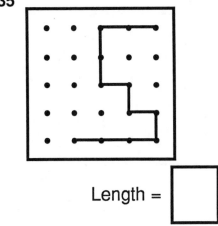

Length = ☐

D–36

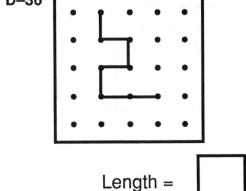

Length = ☐

D–37

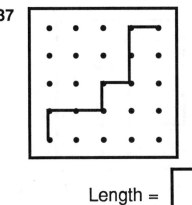

Length = ☐

D–38

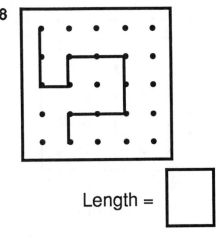

Length = ☐

D–39

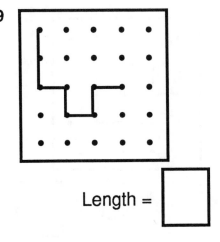

Length = ☐

                                       P.O. BOX 448, PACIFIC GROVE, CA 93950

FINDING LENGTHS OF PATHS

Find the length of each path. Write the answer in the box.
Draw a line between boxes that contain paths that are the same length.

Example:

Length = **11**

D–40

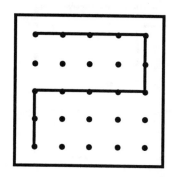

Length = ☐

D–41

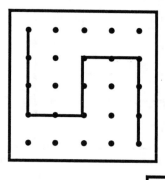

Length = ☐

D–42

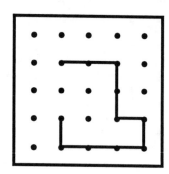

Length = ☐

D–43

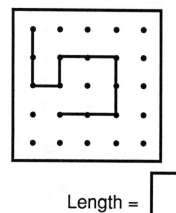

Length = ☐

D–44

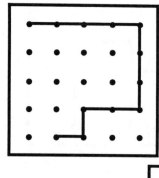

Length = ☐

© 1988 MIDWEST PUBLICATIONS   178   P.O. BOX 448, PACIFIC GROVE, CA 93950

DRAWING PATHS

The length of a path is written in the box.
Draw a path from A to B equal to that length.
Use only horizontal and vertical lines.

Example:

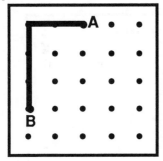

Length = **5**

D–45

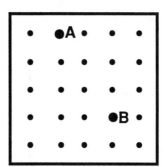

Length = **7**

D–46

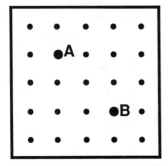

Length = **4**

D–47

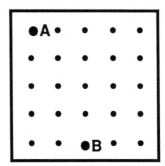

Length = **8**

D–48

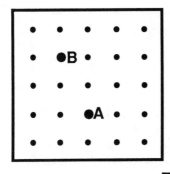

Length = **11**

D–49

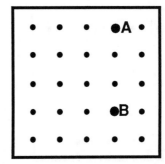

Length = **9**

P.O. BOX 448, PACIFIC GROVE, CA 93950

DRAWING PATHS

Find the length of the path from A to B. Write the answer in the box.
Draw a path from X to B that is the same length.
Use only horizontal and vertical lines.

Example:

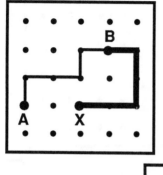

Length = **5**

D–50

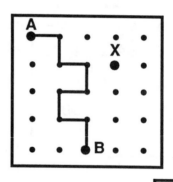

Length = ☐

D–51

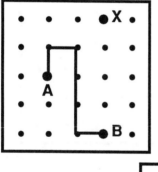

Length = ☐

D–52

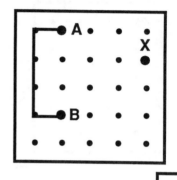

Length = ☐

D–53

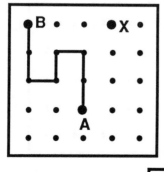

Length = ☐

D–54

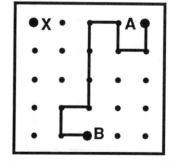

Length = ☐

DRAWING LONGER PATHS

Find the length of the path from A to B. Write the answer in the box.
Draw a path from X to B that is one unit longer than the path from A to B.
Use only horizontal and vertical lines.

Example:

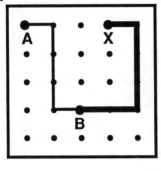

Length = **5**

D–55

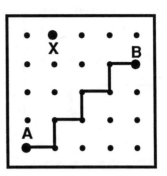

Length = ☐

D–56

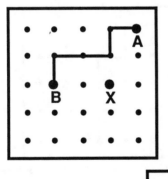

Length = ☐

D–57

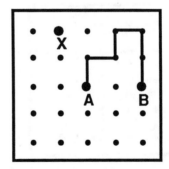

Length = ☐

D–58

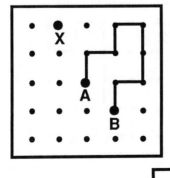

Length = ☐

D–59

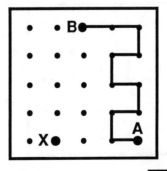

Length = ☐

DRAWING SHORTER PATHS

Find the length of the path from A to B. Write the answer in the box.
Draw a path from X to B that is two units shorter than the path from A to B.
Use only horizontal and vertical lines.

Example:

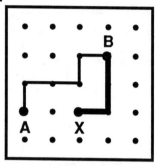

Length = **5**

D–60

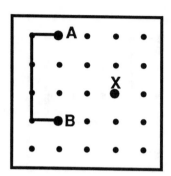

Length = ☐

D–61

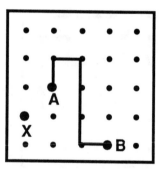

Length = ☐

D–62

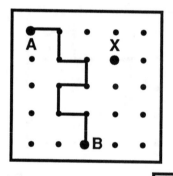

Length = ☐

D–63

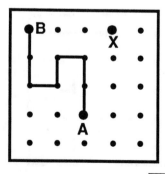

Length = ☐

D–64

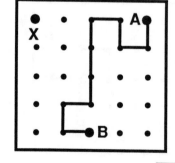

Length = ☐

182   P.O. BOX 448, PACIFIC GROVE, CA 93950

DRAWING PATHS

Find the length of the path from A to B to C. Write the answer in the box.
Draw a path from A to X to C that is the same length.
Use only horizontal and vertical lines.

Example:

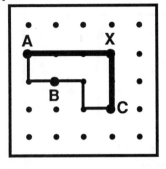

Length = **5**

D–65

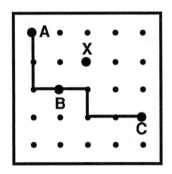

Length = ☐

D–66

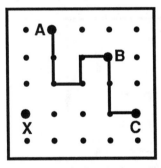

Length = ☐

D–67

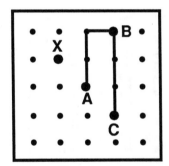

Length = ☐

D–68

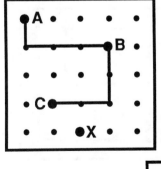

Length = ☐

D–69

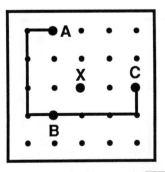

Length = ☐

P.O. BOX 448, PACIFIC GROVE, CA 93950

DRAWING SHORTER PATHS

Find the length of the path from A to B. Write the answer in the box.
Draw a path from A to X to B that is two units shorter.
Use only horizontal and vertical lines.

Example:

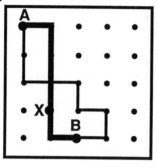

Length = **8**

D–70

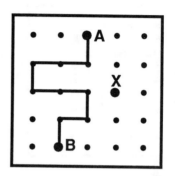

Length = ☐

D–71

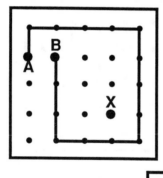

Length = ☐

D–72

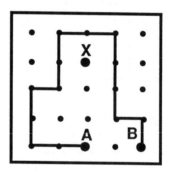

Length = ☐

D–73

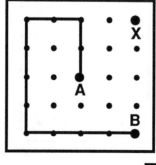

Length = ☐

D–74

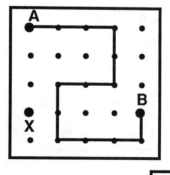

Length = ☐

FINDING LONGER PATHS

One person walks along the dotted path.
Another person walks along the solid path.
Circle the name of the person that walks the longer distance.

Example:

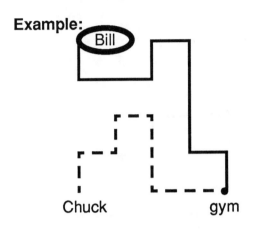

D–75

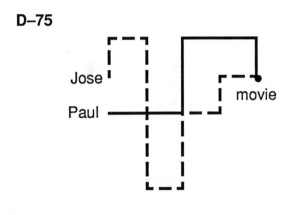

D–76

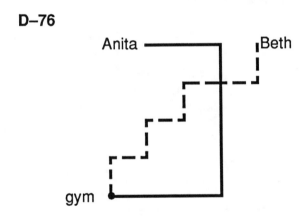

D–77

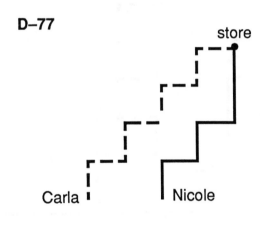

D–78

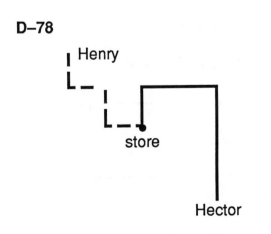

D–79

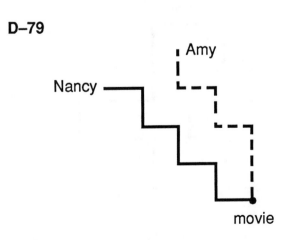

FINDING SHORTER PATHS

One person walks along the dotted path.
Another person walks along the solid path.
Circle the name of the person that walks the shorter distance.

Example: **D–80**

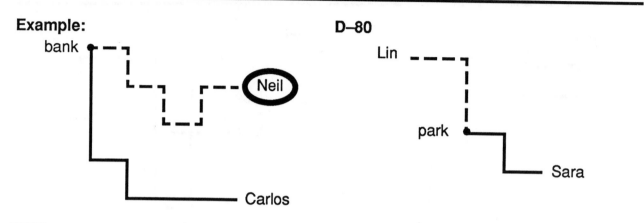

D–81   **D–82**

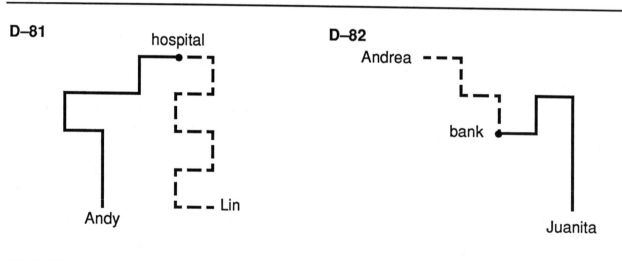

D–83   **D–84**

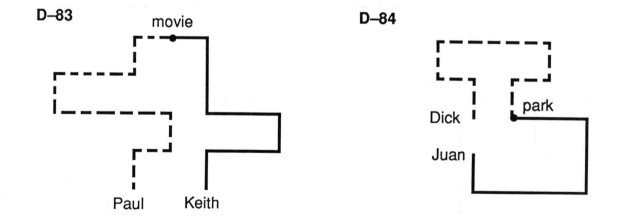

                                       P.O. BOX 448, PACIFIC GROVE, CA 93950

COMPARING PATHS

One person walks along the dotted path.
Another person walks along the solid path.
Circle the name of the person that walks the longer distance.

Example:

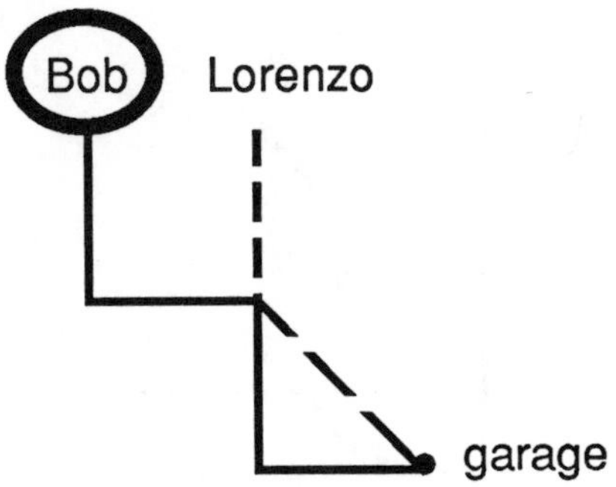

D–85

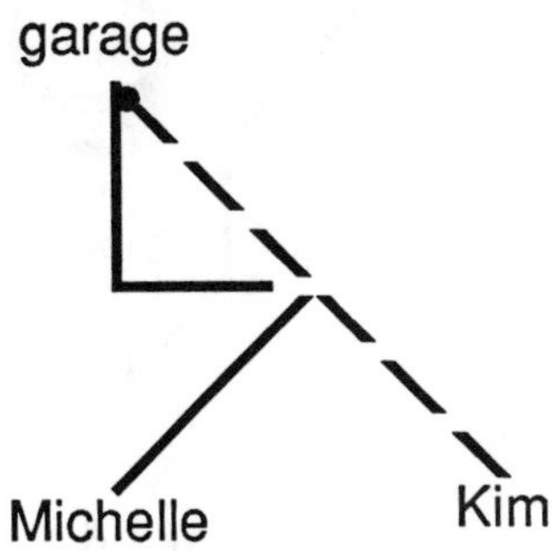

D–86 Which of the four people above has the longest walk to the garage? __________

D–87 Which of the four people above has the shortest walk to the garage? __________

D–88

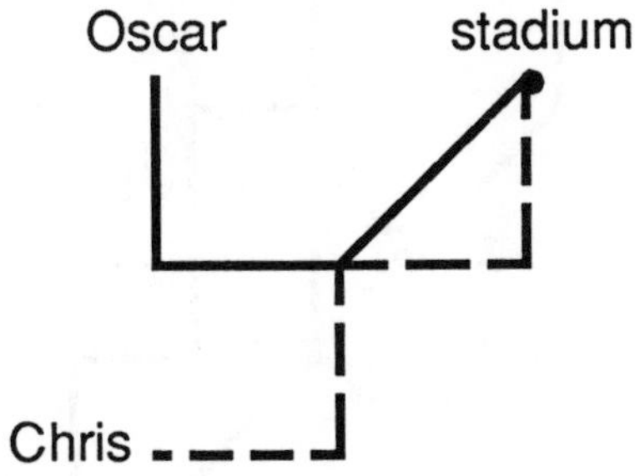

D–89

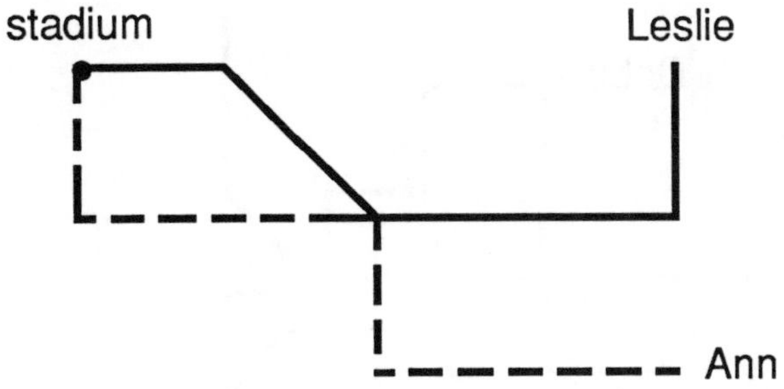

D–90 Which of the four people above has the longest walk to the stadium? __________

D–91 Which of the four people above has the shortest walk to the stadium? __________

COMPARING PATHS

One person walks along the dotted path.
Another person walks along the solid path.
Circle the name of the person that walks the shorter distance.

Example: **D–92**

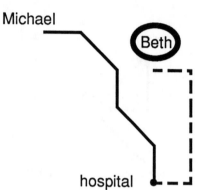

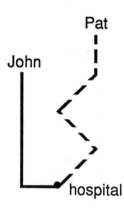

D–93 Which of the four people above has the longest walk to the hospital?_____

D–94 Which of the four people above has the shortest walk to the hospital?_____

D–95   **D–96**

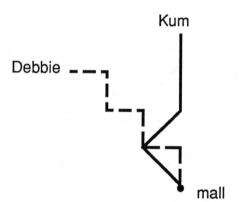

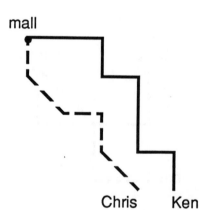

D–97 Which of the four people above has the longest walk to the mall?_____

D–98 Which of the four people above has the shortest walk to the mall?_____

                                                   P.O. BOX 448, PACIFIC GROVE, CA 93950

DISTANCE AROUND FIGURES

Find the distance around each figure.
Write the answer in the box.

Example:

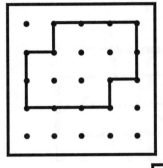

Length = **14**

D–99

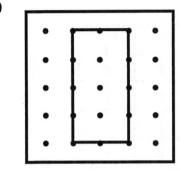

Length = ☐

D–100

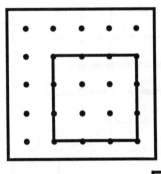

Length = ☐

D–101

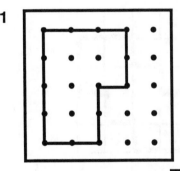

Length = ☐

D–102

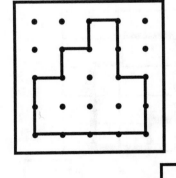

Length = ☐

D–103

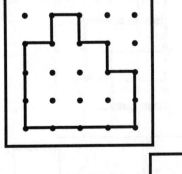

Length = ☐

189   P.O. BOX 448, PACIFIC GROVE, CA 93950

DISTANCE AROUND FIGURES

Find the distance around each figure.
Write the answer in the box.

Example:

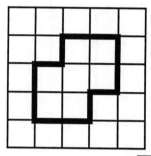

D–104

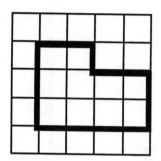

Distance = **12**

Distance =

D–105

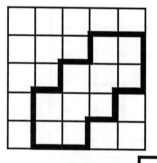

D–106

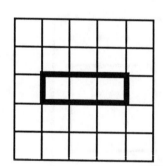

Distance =

Distance =

D–107

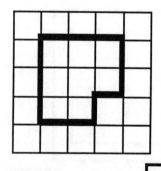

D–108

Distance =

Distance =

                                 P.O. BOX 448, PACIFIC GROVE, CA 93950

DISTANCE AROUND FIGURES

The numbers give the length of each side of the figure.
Match the figure with the distance around the figure.

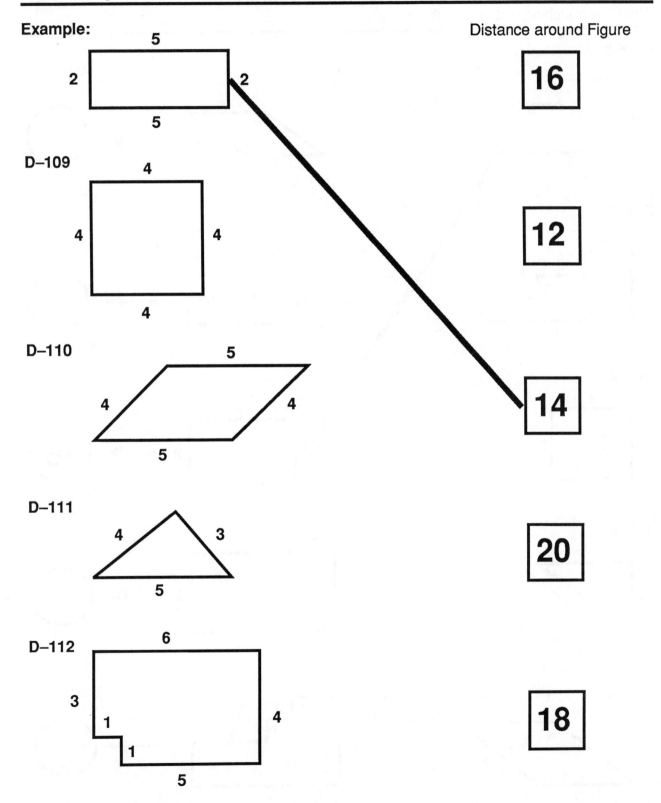

Example:

Distance around Figure

D–109

D–110

D–111

D–112

16

12

14

20

18

DISTANCE AROUND FIGURES

Find the distance around each figure.
Match the figures with the same distance.
Write the matching distance in the circle.

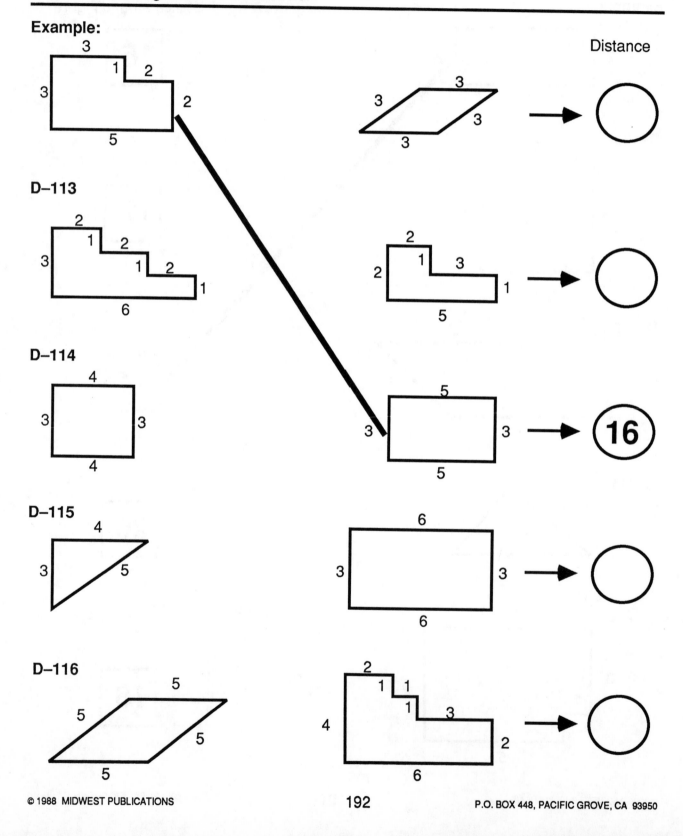

Example:

Distance

D–113

D–114

D–115

D–116

DISTANCES AROUND FIGURES

The figures below are made from one square and one rectangle.
Find the distance around the edges of the new figure.
Do not count the dotted line where the square and rectangle join together.

Example:

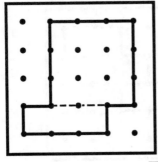

Distance = **16**

D–117

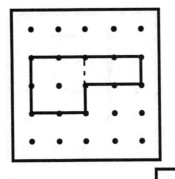

Distance = ☐

D–118

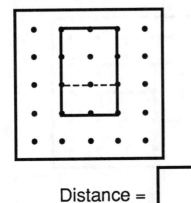

Distance = ☐

D–119

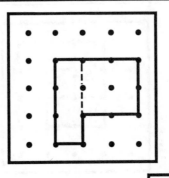

Distance = ☐

D–120

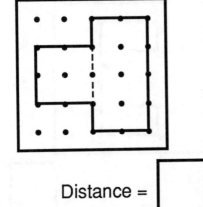

Distance = ☐

D–121

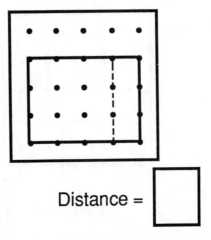

Distance = ☐

© 1988 MIDWEST PUBLICATIONS   P.O. BOX 448, PACIFIC GROVE, CA 93950

DISTANCES AROUND FIGURES

The figures below are made from three rectangles.
Find the distance around the edges of the new figure.
Do not count the dotted lines where the rectangles join together.

Example:

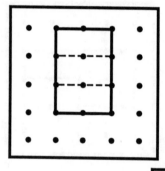

Distance = **10**

D–122

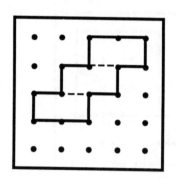

Distance = ☐

D–123

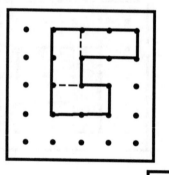

Distance = ☐

D–124

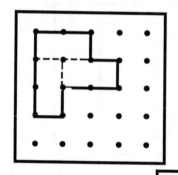

Distance = ☐

D–125

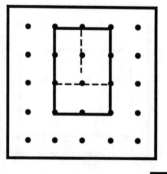

Distance = ☐

D–126

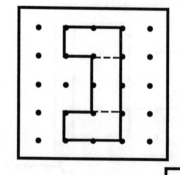

Distance = ☐

P.O. BOX 448, PACIFIC GROVE, CA 93950

DISTANCES AROUND FIGURES

Three rhombuses, like the shaded one, are joined together to make a new figure.
The length of each side is 2.
Find the distance around the edges of each new figure.

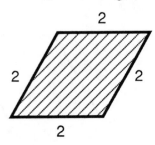

2

2   2

2

Example:

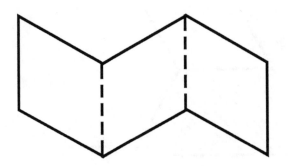

Distance = **16**

D–127

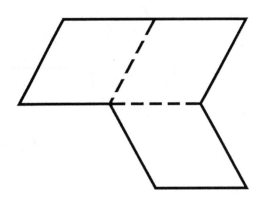

Distance = ☐

D–128

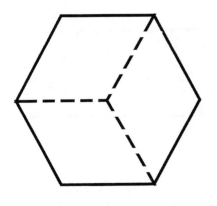

Distance = ☐

D–129

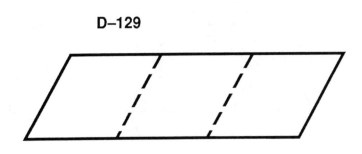

Distance = ☐

DISTANCES AROUND FIGURES

The three shaded shapes below are joined together to make new figures.
The numbers give the lengths of the sides.
Find the distance around the edges of each new figure.

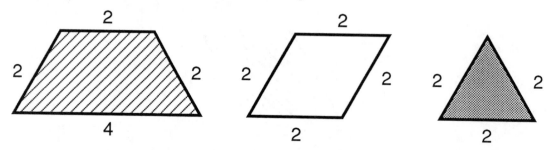

Example: **D–130**

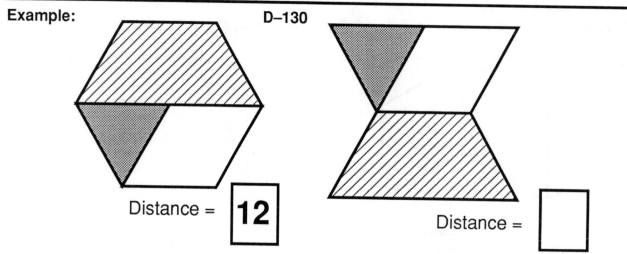

Distance = **12**

Distance = ☐

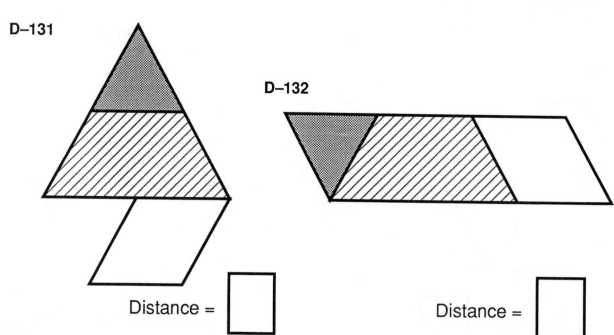

D–131

D–132

Distance = ☐

Distance = ☐

DRAWING FIGURES

The distance around each figure is written in the box.
Complete each figure to match that distance.
Use only horizontal and vertical lines.

Example:

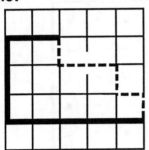

Distance = **16**

D–133

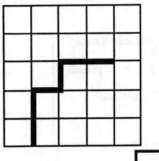

Distance = **12**

D–134

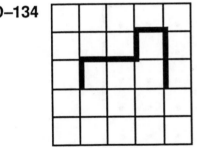

Distance = **10**

D–135

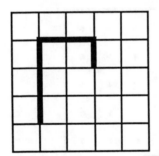

Distance = **14**

D–136

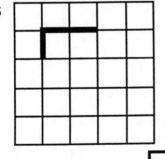

Distance = **8**

D–137

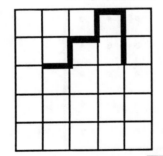

Distance = **18**

P.O. BOX 448, PACIFIC GROVE, CA 93950

DRAWING FIGURES

The distance around a figure is written in the box.
Draw a figure with the distance indicated in each box.
Use only horizontal and vertical lines.

Example:

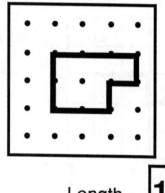

Length = **10**

D–138

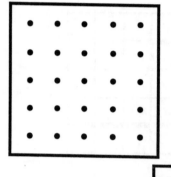

Length = **14**

D–139

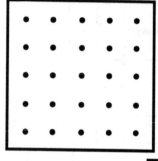

Length = **16**

D–140

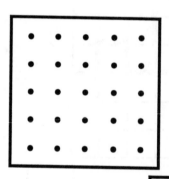

Length = **8**

D–141

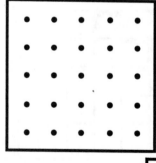

Length = **18**

D–142

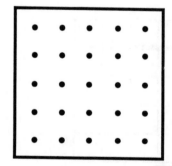

Length = **12**

P.O. BOX 448, PACIFIC GROVE, CA 93950

FINDING MISSING LENGTHS

The numbers give the length of some sides of the figure.
Write the missing lengths in the circles.

Example: **D–143**

D–144   **D–145**

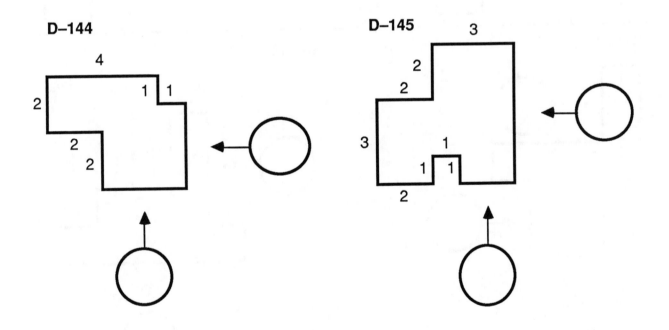

FINDING MISSING LENGTHS

Write the missing lengths in the circles.
Find the distance around the figure.
Write the distance in the box.

Example:

D–146

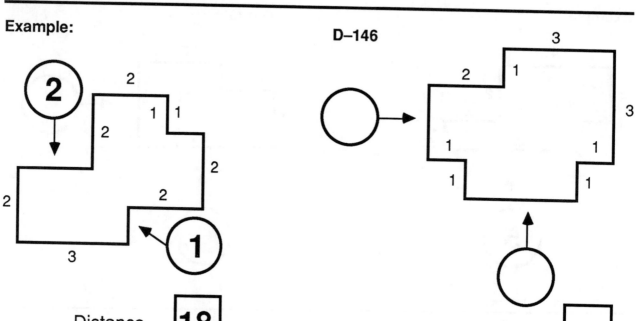

Distance = **18**

D–147

D–148

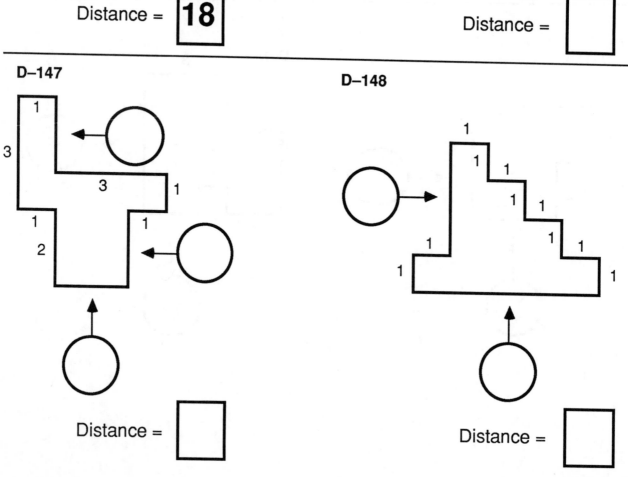

Distance =

Distance =

P.O. BOX 448, PACIFIC GROVE, CA 93950

FINDING AREA BY COUNTING

Count the number of squares in each figure.
Place the answer in the Area box.

Example:

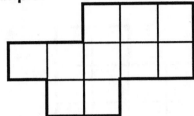

Area = **10**

D–149

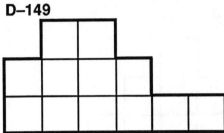

Area =

D–150

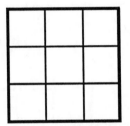

Area =

D–151

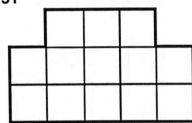

Area =

D–152

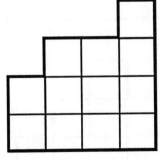

Area =

D–153

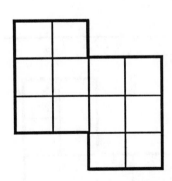

Area =

P.O. BOX 448, PACIFIC GROVE, CA 93950

FINDING AREA BY COUNTING

Count the number of squares in each figure.
Place the answer in the Area box.

Example:

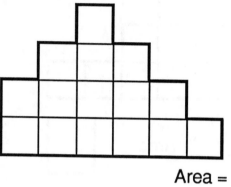

Area = **15**

D–154

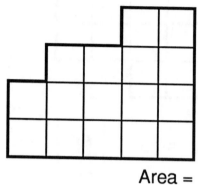

Area =

D–155

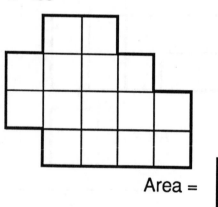

Area =

D–156

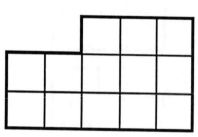

Area =

D–157

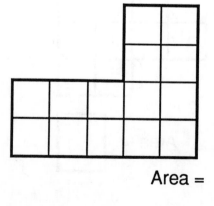

Area =

D–158

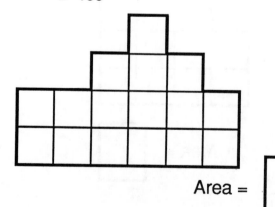

Area =

PATTERN COUNTING

Count the number of squares in each row or column.
Write the answer on the blank indicated by the arrow.
Write the total number of squares in the circle.

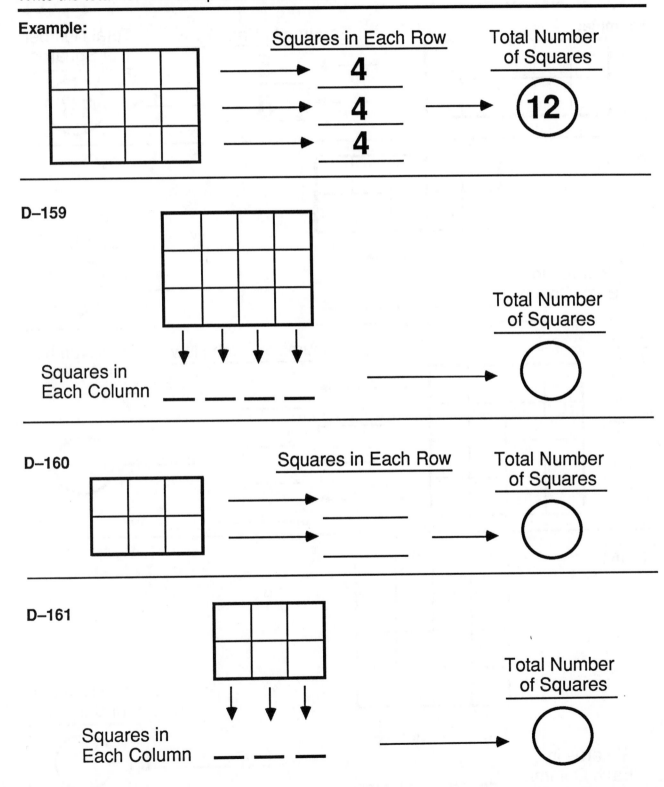

Example:

Squares in Each Row

4
4
4

Total Number of Squares

(12)

D–159

Total Number of Squares

Squares in
Each Column ___ ___ ___ ___

D–160

Squares in Each Row

Total Number of Squares

D–161

Squares in
Each Column ___ ___ ___

Total Number of Squares

P.O. BOX 448, PACIFIC GROVE, CA 93950

PATTERN COUNTING

Count the number of squares in each row or column.
Write the answer on the blank indicated by the arrow.
Write the total number of squares in the circle.

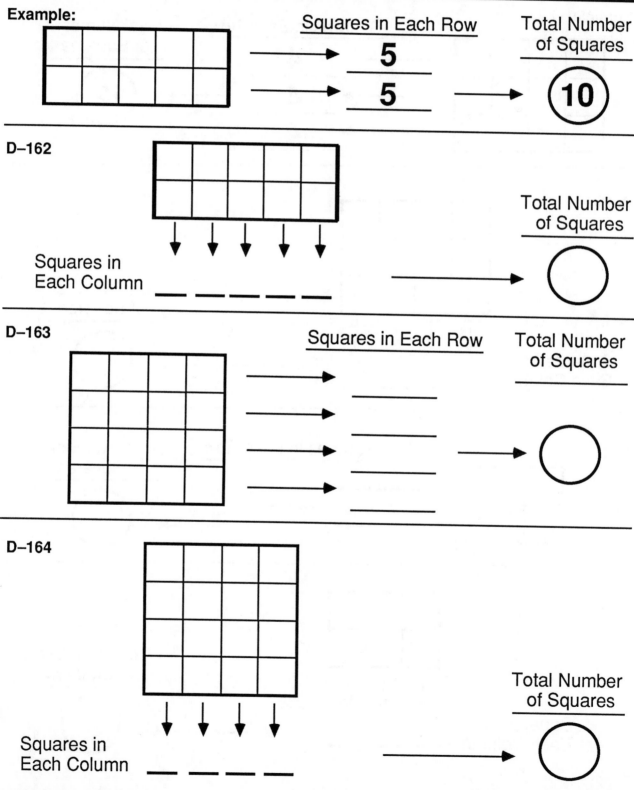

Example:

Squares in Each Row

→ **5**

→ **5**

Total Number
of Squares

→ (**10**)

D–162

Total Number
of Squares

Squares in
Each Column ___ ___ ___ ___ ___

D–163

Squares in Each Row

Total Number
of Squares

D–164

Total Number
of Squares

Squares in
Each Column ___ ___ ___ ___

204   P.O. BOX 448, PACIFIC GROVE, CA 93950

FINDING AREA BY COUNTING

Count the number of squares in each figure.

Example:

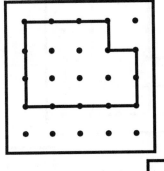

Area = **11**

D–165

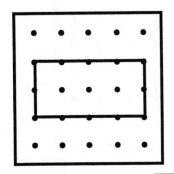

Area =

D–166

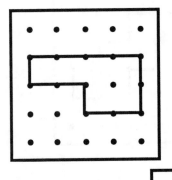

Area =

D–167

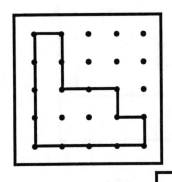

Area =

D–168

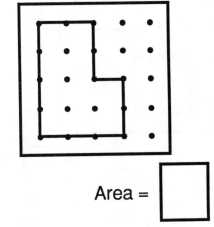

Area =

D–169

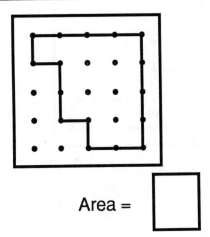

Area =

205   P.O. BOX 448, PACIFIC GROVE, CA 93950

FINDING AREA BY COUNTING

Count the number of squares in each figure.

D–170

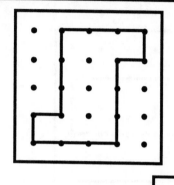

Area = ☐

D–171

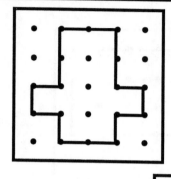

Area = ☐

D–172

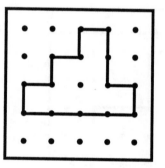

Area = ☐

D–173

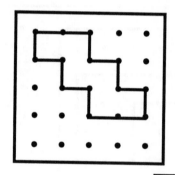

Area = ☐

D–174

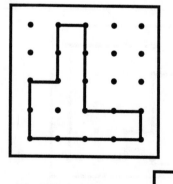

Area = ☐

D–175

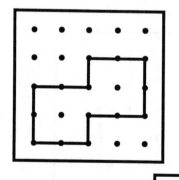

Area = ☐

                                       P.O. BOX 448, PACIFIC GROVE, CA 93950

COMPLETING THE RECTANGLE

Add lines to each figure to make it into one rectangle.
Find the number of squares needed to complete the rectangle.

Example:

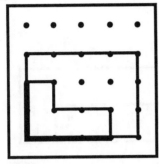

D–176

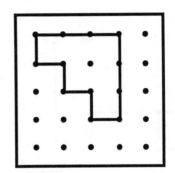

Number of
squares needed = **4**

Number of
squares needed =

D–177

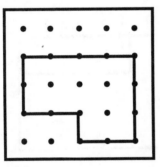

D–178

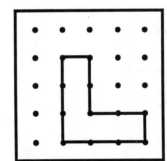

Number of
squares needed =

Number of
squares needed =

D–179

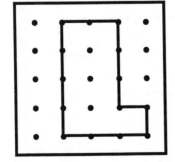

D–180

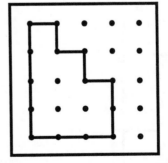

Number of
squares needed =

Number of
squares needed =

207   P.O. BOX 448, PACIFIC GROVE, CA 93950

COMPLETING THE RECTANGLE

The numbers give the lengths of the edges.
The dotted lines complete the rectangle.
Find the number of squares needed to complete the rectangle.

Example:

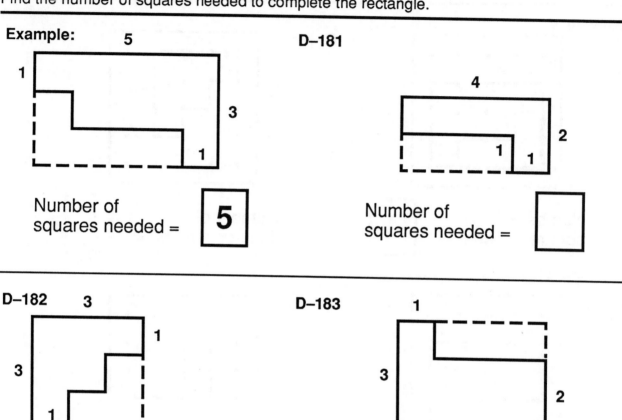

Number of
squares needed = **5**

D–181

Number of
squares needed =

D–182

Number of
squares needed =

D–183

Number of
squares needed =

D–184

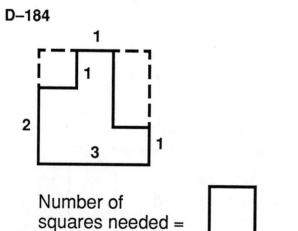

Number of
squares needed =

D–185

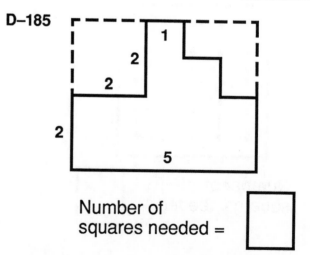

Number of
squares needed =

FINDING AREA BY COUNTING

Units are marked on the edges of the figures.
Connect the marks to divide the figures into squares.
Count the number of squares in each figure.

Example:

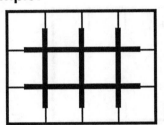

Area = **12**

D–186

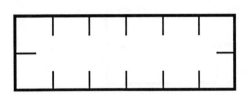

Area =

D–187

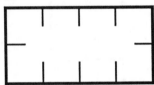

Area =

D–188

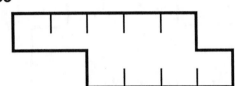

Area =

D–189

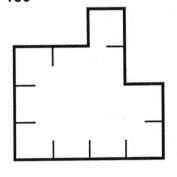

Area =

D–190

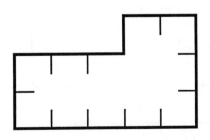

Area =

P.O. BOX 448, PACIFIC GROVE, CA 93950

FINDING AREA BY COUNTING

Units are marked on the edges of the figures.
Connect the marks to divide the figures into squares.
Count the number of squares in each figure.

D–191

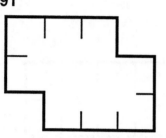

D–192

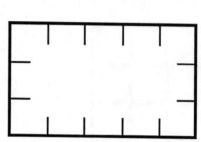

Area = [ ]   Area = [ ]

D–193

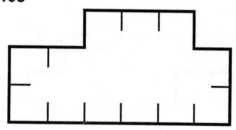

D–194

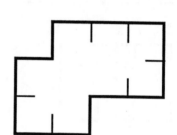

Area = [ ]   Area = [ ]

D–195

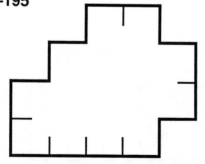

D–196

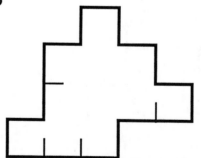

Area = [ ]   Area = [ ]

COMPUTING AREA

The square is divided into four regions.

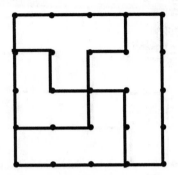

Find each figure in the square.
Write the area of the figure in the box.

Example:

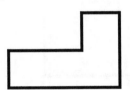

Area = **4**

D–197

Area =

D–198

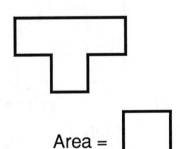

Area =

D–199

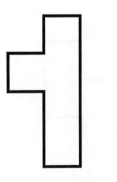

Area =

P.O. BOX 448, PACIFIC GROVE, CA 93950

COMPUTING AREA

The rectangle is divided into six regions.

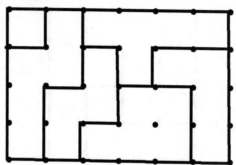

Find each figure in the rectangle.
Write the area of the figure in the box.

D–200

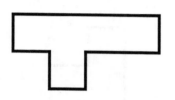

Area = ☐

D–201

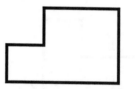

Area = ☐

D–202

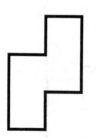

Area = ☐

D–203

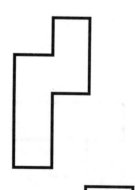

Area = ☐

                                  P.O. BOX 448, PACIFIC GROVE, CA 93950

COMPUTING AREA

The square is divided into five regions.
The numbers give the area of each region.

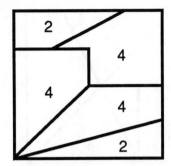

Each figure below can be found in the square.
Find the area of each figure.
Write the area of the figure in the box.

Example: **D–204**

Area = **2**   Area =

D–205   **D–206**

Area =   Area =

                                P.O. BOX 448, PACIFIC GROVE, CA 93950

COMPUTING AREA

The square is divided into five regions.
The numbers give the area of each region.

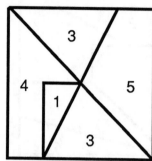

Each figure below can be found in the square.
Find the area of each figure.
Write the area in the box.

Example: **D–207**

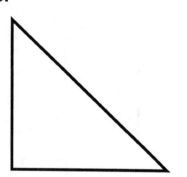

Area = **8**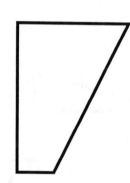

Area = ☐

D–208   **D–209**

   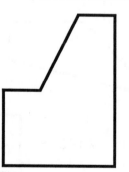

Area = ☐   Area = ☐

---

214   P.O. BOX 448, PACIFIC GROVE, CA 93950

AREA USING 1/2 UNITS

The area of the square is 1.   ⟶

This square is divided into two triangles.   ⟶
The area of one triangle is 1/2.

Divide each figure below into squares and half-squares.
Write the answers in the boxes.

Example:

Number of squares = **6**

Number of 1/2 squares = **2**

Area = **7**

D–210

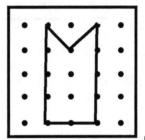

Number of squares = ☐

Number of 1/2 squares = ☐

Area = ☐

D–211

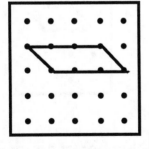

Number of squares = ☐

Number of 1/2 squares = ☐

Area = ☐

D–212

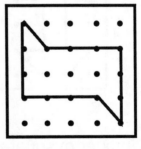

Number of squares = ☐

Number of 1/2 squares = ☐

Area = ☐

       P.O. BOX 448, PACIFIC GROVE, CA 93950

AREA USING 1/2 UNITS

Divide each figure into squares and half-squares.
Write the answers in the boxes.

D–213

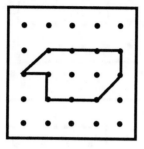

Number of squares = ☐

Number of 1/2 squares = ☐

Area = ☐

D–214

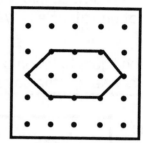

Number of squares = ☐

Number of 1/2 squares = ☐

Area = ☐

D–215

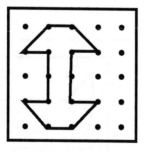

Number of squares = ☐

Number of 1/2 squares = ☐

Area = ☐

D–216

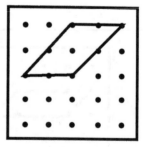

Number of squares = ☐

Number of 1/2 squares = ☐

Area = ☐

                                       P.O. BOX 448, PACIFIC GROVE, CA 93950

DRAWING FIGURES

The area is written in the box.
Draw a figure with that area.

Example:

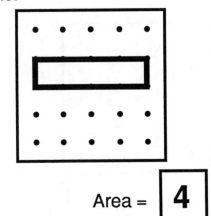

Area = 4

D–217

Area = 6

D–218

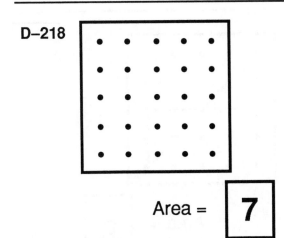

Area = 7

D–219

Area = 8

D–220

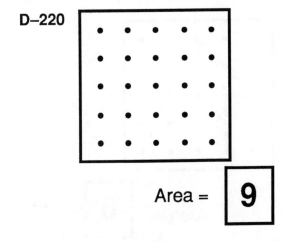

Area = 9

D–221

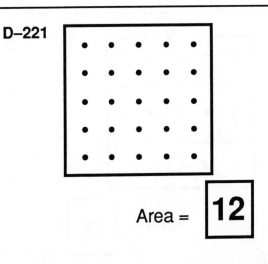

Area = 12

P.O. BOX 448, PACIFIC GROVE, CA 93950

DRAWING FIGURES

The area is written in the box.
Part of a figure has been drawn.
Complete the figure with that area.

Example:

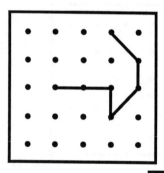

Area = **7**

D–222

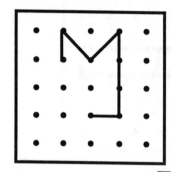

Area = **6**

D–223

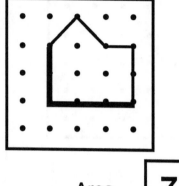

Area = **7**

D–224

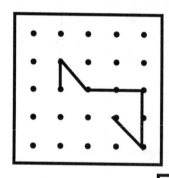

Area = **5**

D–225

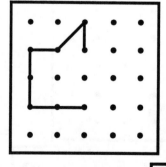

Area = **5**

D–226

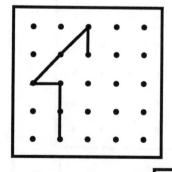

Area = **6**

                                       P.O. BOX 448, PACIFIC GROVE, CA 93950

ESTIMATING AREA

Circle the number you think is closest to the area of the figure.

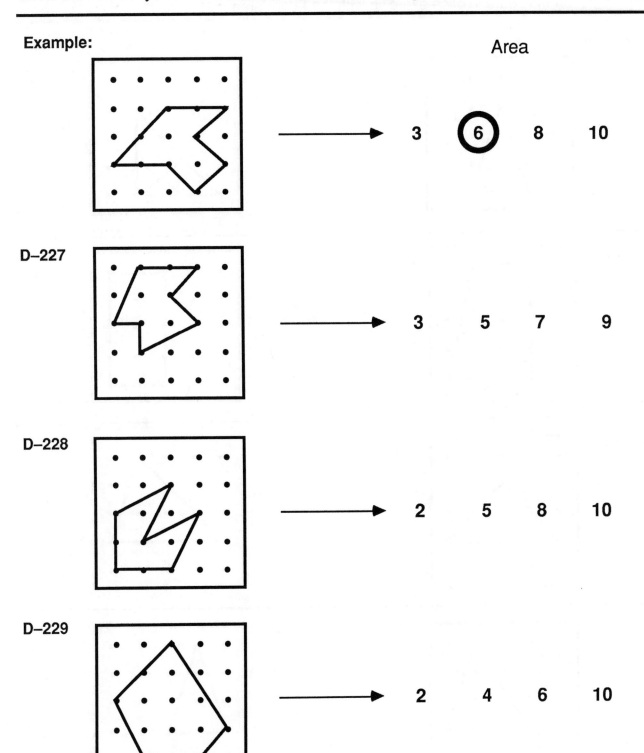

Example: Area

3   (6)   8   10

D–227

3   5   7   9

D–228

2   5   8   10

D–229

2   4   6   10

                                 P.O. BOX 448, PACIFIC GROVE, CA 93950

ESTIMATING AREA

Put an ✕ on the figure in each exercise with the larger area.

Example:

 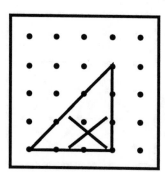

D–230

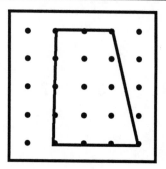 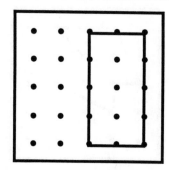

D–231

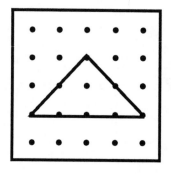 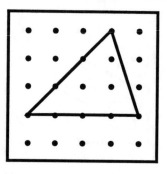

D–232

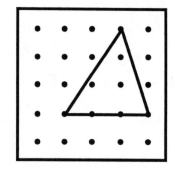 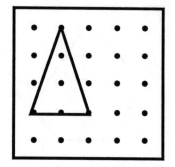

220   P.O. BOX 448, PACIFIC GROVE, CA 93950

WHAT COMPUTATION DO YOU USE?

Circle the computation that solves the problem.

Example:

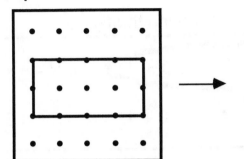

The area of the figure is

4 + 2	$\boxed{2 \times 4}$
4 + 2 + 4 + 2	3 × 5
3 + 5	3 + 5 + 3 + 5

D–233

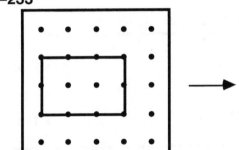

The distance around the figure is

3 + 2	3 × 2
3 + 2 + 3 + 2	4 × 3
4 + 3	4 + 3 + 4 + 3

D–234

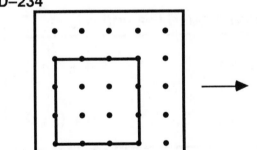

The area of the figure is

3 + 3	3 × 3
3 + 3 + 3 + 3	4 × 4
4 + 4	4 + 4 + 4 + 4

D–235

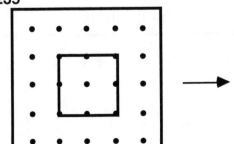

The distance around the figure is

2 + 2	2 × 2
2 + 2 + 2 + 2	3 × 3
3 + 3	3 + 3 + 3 + 4

WHAT COMPUTATION DO YOU USE?

Circle the computation that solves the problem.

Example:

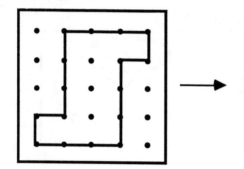

The distance around the figure is

$$\boxed{3 + 1 + 1 + 3 + 3 + 1 + 1 + 3} \qquad 3 \times 4$$

$$4 + 2 + 2 + 4 + 4 + 2 + 2 + 4 \qquad 3 \times 1 \times 3$$

D–236

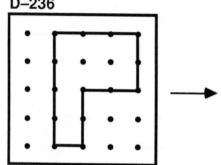

The area of the figure is

$$3 + 2 + 2 + 2 + 1 + 4 \qquad 3 + 3 + 2$$

$$4 + 3 + 3 + 3 + 2 + 5 \qquad 4 + 4 + 3$$

D–237

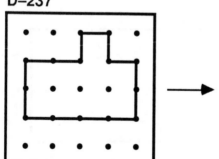

The distance around the figure is

$$1 + 1 + 1 + 1 + 2 + 4 + 2 + 2 \qquad 4 + 4 + 1$$

$$2 + 2 + 2 + 2 + 3 + 5 + 3 + 3 \qquad 5 + 5 + 2$$

D–238

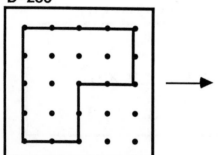

The area of the figure is

$$4 + 2 + 2 + 2 + 2 + 4 \qquad 4 + 4 + 2 + 2$$

$$5 + 3 + 3 + 3 + 3 + 5 \qquad 5 + 5 + 3 + 3$$

222   P.O. BOX 448, PACIFIC GROVE, CA 93950

COMPARING NUMBERS

Circle the largest number in each set.
Draw a line under the smallest number.

Example:

3	(8)	7
4	5	2

E–1

8	1	5
9	7	3

E–2

23	18	10
9	8	21
15	19	6

E–3

12	22	8
5	16	27
18	11	14

E–4

103	98	93
115	167	144
95	135	163

E–5

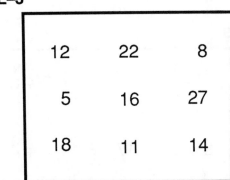

263	135	422
342	208	195
482	190	364

E–6   Which is the largest number in all the sets? _____

E–7   Which is the smallest number in all the sets? _____

223   P.O. BOX 448, PACIFIC GROVE, CA 93950

COMPARING NUMBERS

Circle the largest value in each set.
Draw a line under the smallest value.

Example:

3 + 5	8 + 6	(8 + 7)
4 + 4	3 + 4	7 + 7

E–8

8 + 9	6 + 2	8 + 8
6 + 3	5 + 4	9 + 9

E–9

17 − 3	16 − 8	7 + 6
8 + 5	17 − 8	8 + 4

E–10

7 × 5	9 + 7	7 × 4
6 × 5	9 + 8	9 + 6

E–11

8 × 2	6 × 5	42 ÷ 7
27 ÷ 3	5 × 3	49 + 7

E–12

30 ÷ 6	12 + 6	56 ÷ 7
6 × 3	12 + 8	4 × 3

E–13 Which is the largest value in all the sets?_____

E–14 Which is the smallest value in all the sets?_____

P.O. BOX 448, PACIFIC GROVE, CA 93950

ORDERING NUMBERS

The symbols below are used to compare numbers.
Write the correct symbol in the box.

is greater than	is less than	is equal to
>	<	=

Example:

12 | < | 13

E–15

9 | ☐ | 8

E–16

23 | ☐ | 32

E–17

16 | ☐ | 10 + 6

E–18

16 + 9 | ☐ | 16

E–19

17 − 9 | ☐ | 17

E–20

15 | ☐ | 8 + 7

E–21

24 − 9 | ☐ | 10

E–22

16 − 8 | ☐ | 8

E–23

8 + 16 | ☐ | 19

ORDERING NUMBERS

The symbols below are used to compare numbers.
Circle the number that belongs in the circle.

is greater than	is less than	is equal to
>	**<**	**=**

Example:

$16 <$ ◯

a. 15
b. 16
c. **(17)**

E–24

$45 <$ ◯

a. 46
b. 44
c. 45

E–25

$47 >$ ◯

a. $24 + 26$
b. $23 + 22$
c. $25 + 25$

E–26

$34 =$ ◯

a. $17 + 18$
b. $16 + 14$
c. $16 + 18$

E–27

◯ > 26

a. $15 + 10$
b. $13 + 13$
c. $15 + 14$

E–28

◯ < 49

a. 6×7
b. $25 + 25$
c. 7×7

E–29

$12 + 8 < 12 +$ ◯

a. 7
b. 9
c. 8

E–30

$18 +$ ◯ $= 17 + 16$

a. 18
b. 15
c. 17

E–31

$9 + 8 < 9 +$ ◯

a. 8
b. 9
c. 6

E–32

$12 + 14 =$ ◯

a. $13 + 13$
b. $12 + 15$
c. $13 + 14$

ORDERING NUMBERS

The symbols below are used to compare numbers.
Circle the numbers that belong in the circle.

is greater than   **is less than**

>   **<**

Example: **E–33**

$< 9 < 12$ $18 < 21 <$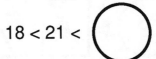

| 10 | (5) | (7) | 14 |

| 19 | 25 | 34 | 16 |

E–34   **E–35**

$< 27 < 43$ $25 > 9 >$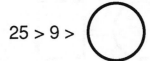

| 19 | 23 | 29 | 6 |

| 18 | 26 | 8 | 10 |

E–36   **E–37**

$12 >$ ◯ > 8 $20 >$ ◯ > 10

| 11 | 9 | 7 | 13 |

| 9 | 20 | 19 | 15 |

E–38   **E–39**

$35 <$ ◯ < 45 $50 >$ ◯ > 10

| 34 | 47 | 35 | 36 |

| 15 | 20 | 35 | 5 |

227   P.O. BOX 448, PACIFIC GROVE, CA 93950

ORDERING NUMBERS

Fill in the shapes with the three numbers to make a true sentence.

Example:

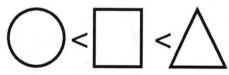

| 6 | 9 | 4 |

E–40

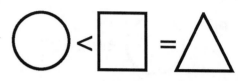

| 8 | 8 | 3 |

E–41

| 5 | 17 | 5 |

E–42

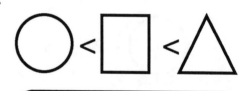

| 12 | 8 | 16 |

E–43

| 11 | 23 | 16 |

E–44

| 35 | 21 | 13 |

E–45

| 7 | 9 | 7 |

E–46

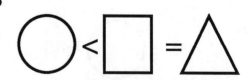

| 40 | 40 | 36 |

USING THE ORDER RELATIONS

Draw a line around the true sentence.

Example:

$4 \times 5 < 20$

$\boxed{4 \times 5 = 20}$

$4 \times 5 > 20$

E–47

$6 \times 5 = 25$

$6 \times 5 < 25$

$6 \times 5 > 25$

E–48

$9 + 8 < 15$

$9 + 8 > 15$

$9 + 8 = 15$

E–49

$18 - 7 < 18$

$18 - 7 > 18$

$18 \times 7 = 18$

E–50

$15 + 12 = 28$

$16 + 12 = 28$

$16 + 13 < 28$

E–51

$14 < 13 + 3$

$14 > 13 + 3$

$14 < 13 - 3$

E–52

$6 + 4 > 10$

$7 \times 5 < 12$

$17 - 7 > 7$

E–53

$100 < 16 + 32$

$50 > 50 - 32$

$40 > 40 \times 3$

P.O. BOX 448, PACIFIC GROVE, CA 93950

USING THE ORDER RELATIONS

Write the correct symbol in the box.

is greater than	is less than	is equal to
>	**<**	**=**

Example:

$3 + 4$ $\boxed{<}$ 12

$3 + 4$ $\boxed{>}$ 5

$3 + 4$ $\boxed{=}$ 7

E–54

$5 + 6$ $\square$ 11

$5 + 7$ $\square$ 11

5×7 $\square$ 11

E–55

9×9 $\square$ 18

$9 + 9$ $\square$ 18

$9 - 9$ $\square$ 18

E–56

4 $\square$ $12 - 6$

7 $\square$ $12 - 6$

5 $\square$ $12 - 6$

E–57

20 $\square$ $13 + 7$

20 $\square$ $7 + 13$

20 $\square$ $13 - 7$

E–58

$19 + 7$ $\square$ 27

$8 + 19$ $\square$ 27

$18 + 19$ $\square$ 27

E–59

$23 + 23$ $\square$ 60

$37 + 15$ $\square$ 60

15×4 $\square$ 60

E–60

90 $\square$ $43 + 43$

90 $\square$ 43×2

90 $\square$ $43 - 43$

USING ORDER RELATIONS

A number is missing from each sentence.
Circle all the numbers that will make a true sentence.

Example:

$10 + \bigcirc > 12$

| ③ | 1 | 2 | ⑤ |

E–61

$16 > \bigcirc + 6$

| 10 | 11 | 16 | 9 |

E–62

$17 - \bigcirc < 10$

| 7 | 6 | 10 | 8 |

E–63

$8 = 8 - \bigcirc$

| 8 | 7 | 0 | 1 |

E–64

$27 < 9 \times \bigcirc$

| 3 | 4 | 2 | 8 |

E–65

$8 \times \bigcirc < 48$

| 6 | 5 | 10 | 8 |

E–66

$63 < 60 + \bigcirc$

| 13 | 10 | 2 | 3 |

E–67

$16 \times \bigcirc > 32$

| 1 | 2 | 3 | 4 |

© 1988 MIDWEST PUBLICATIONS   P.O. BOX 448, PACIFIC GROVE, CA 93950

USING ORDER RELATIONS

A number is missing from each sentence.
Circle all the numbers that will make a true sentence.

E–68

$8 + \bigcirc < 15$

(② ③ ⑥ 7 9)

E–69

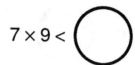

(43 53 63 73 83)

E–70

$16 - 5 < 16 - \bigcirc$

(2 3 5 7 9)

E–71

$12 - 7 > \bigcirc$

(0 2 5 7 9)

E–72

$4 + \bigcirc > 4 + 5$

(2 3 4 5 7)

E–73

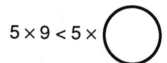

(8 9 10 12 16)

E–74

$24 - \bigcirc < 24 - 13$

(5 7 13 17 19)

E–75

(0 4 6 16 24)

             P.O. BOX 448, PACIFIC GROVE, CA 93950

USING ARITHMETIC OPERATIONS

Circle the operation that makes the sentence true.
Write the symbol of that operation in the box.

Example:

$9\ \boxed{+}\ 8 = 17$

$\left(\ \textcircled{+}\quad \times \quad \div \quad - \ \right)$

E–76

$12 > 24\ \boxed{}\ 13$

$\left(\ -\qquad\qquad + \ \right)$

E–77

$15\ \boxed{}\ 3 > 20$

$\left(\ \times\qquad\qquad + \ \right)$

E–78

$36 < 9\ \boxed{}\ 5$

$\left(\ +\quad \times \quad - \ \right)$

E–79

$18\ \boxed{}\ 3 = 6$

$\left(\ +\quad -\quad \div \ \right)$

E–80

$27\ \boxed{}\ 3 < 27$

$\left(\ +\quad -\quad \times \ \right)$

E–81

$10 > 45\ \boxed{}\ 5$

$\left(\ +\quad \times \quad -\quad \div \ \right)$

E–82

$32 = 320\ \boxed{}\ 10$

$\left(\ +\quad \times \quad \div \quad - \ \right)$

P.O. BOX 448, PACIFIC GROVE, CA 93950

USING ARITHMETIC OPERATIONS

The four arithmetic operations are listed below.
Write one operation in the box that makes the sentence true.

$$+ \quad - \quad \times \quad \div$$

Example:

$9 \boxed{\times} 3 > 20$

E–83

$90 < 38 \boxed{} 19$

E–84

$27 < 25 \boxed{} 5$

E–85

$77 \boxed{} 11 > 30$

E–86

$27 \boxed{} 9 > 30$

E–87

$56 \boxed{} 7 = 8$

E–88

$48 \boxed{} 6 < 9$

E–89

$17 = 27 \boxed{} 10$

E–90

$70 < 18 \boxed{} 9$

E–91

$24 \boxed{} 3 > 42$

MAKING TRUE SENTENCES

The first number in each pair is a box number.
The second number is a circle number.
Circle all the pairs that will make the sentence true.

Example: $\Box + \bigcirc = 12$

a. (7, 5)   b. (4, 8)

c. 6, 7   d. 5, 8

E–92 $\Box + \bigcirc > 16$

a. 7, 9   b. 8, 9

c. 9, 9   d. 8, 8

E–93 $46 > \bigcirc \times \Box$

a. 6, 7   b. 6, 6

c. 7, 7   d. 6, 8

E–94 $\Box - \bigcirc = 9$

a. 13, 6   b. 13, 5

c. 18, 8   d. 17, 8

E–95 $8 < \bigcirc \div \Box$

a. 48, 8   b. 63, 7

c. 48, 6   d. 64, 8

E–96 $\Box \times \bigcirc < 50$

a. 7, 7   b. 7, 8

c. 8, 8   d. 6, 9

                      P.O. BOX 448, PACIFIC GROVE, CA 93950

MAKING TRUE SENTENCES

The first number in each pair is a box number. The second number is a circle number.
Use the numbers from two of the pairs to make the sentences true.
Draw arrows to show which pairs go with the sentences.

Example:

　a.　3, 4

　b.　5, 5

　c.　3, 5

$8 + \boxed{5} > 7 + \bigcirc{5}$

$8 + \boxed{3} < 7 + \bigcirc{5}$

E–97

　a.　9, 2

　b.　2, 9

　c.　0, 3

$\boxed{} \times 9 = \bigcirc{} + 9$

$\boxed{} \times 9 > \bigcirc{} + 9$

E–98

　a.　24, 3

　b.　18, 3

　c.　6, 6

$\boxed{} \div 3 > 18 \div \bigcirc{}$

$\boxed{} \div 3 < 18 \div \bigcirc{}$

E–99

　a.　23, 23

　b.　5, 12

　c.　12, 5

$12 + \boxed{} > \bigcirc{} + 12$

$12 + \boxed{} = \bigcirc{} + 12$

E–100

　a.　24, 48

　b.　48, 24

　c.　24, 24

$54 - \boxed{} > 54 - \bigcirc{}$

$54 - \boxed{} < 54 - \bigcirc{}$

　　　　　　　　　　　　P.O. BOX 448, PACIFIC GROVE, CA 93950

SEQUENCES OF NUMBERS

The numbers on the left <u>begin</u> a sequence.
Circle the row on the right that <u>continues</u> the sequence.

Example:

     1, 3, 5, 7, 9,

     a.   10, 11, 12, 13

     b.   9, 11, 13, 15

     c.   (11, 13, 15, 17)

E–101

     1, 4, 7, 10, 13,

     a.   15, 18, 21, 24

     b.   16, 19, 22, 25

     c.   14, 15, 16, 17

E–102

     1, 2, 1, 3, 1, 4,

     a.   1, 5, 1, 6

     b.   5, 1, 6, 1

     c.   4, 1, 5, 1

E–103

     45, 40, 35, 30,

     a.   35, 40, 45, 50

     b.   20, 15, 10, 5

     c.   25, 20, 15, 10

E–104

     2, 1, 4, 3, 6, 5, 8, 7,

     a.   7, 10, 9, 12

     b.   8, 9, 10, 11

     c.   10, 9, 12, 11

P.O. BOX 448, PACIFIC GROVE, CA 93950

SEQUENCES OF NUMBERS

The numbers on the right <u>end</u> a sequence.
Circle the row on the left that <u>begins</u> the sequence.

Example: a.   18, 20, 22, 24,

                b.   (2, 4, 6, 8,)   10, 12, 14, 16

                c.   41, 6, 8, 10,

E–105   a.   33, 37, 41, 45,

                b.   3, 7, 11, 15,   17, 21, 25, 29

                c.   1, 5, 9, 13,

E–106   a.   6, 9, 12, 15,

                b.   39, 36, 33, 30,   18, 21, 24, 27

                c.   3, 6, 19, 12,

E–107   a.   25, 30, 35, 40,

                b.   40, 35, 30, 25,   20, 15, 10, 5

                c.   30, 35, 40, 45,

E–108   a.   26, 29, 32, 35,

                b.   3, 6, 9, 12,   14, 17, 20, 23

                c.   2, 5, 8, 11,

SEQUENCES OF NUMBERS

Each sequence has missing numbers.
Fill in the blanks.

Example: **6**, **9**, 12, 15, 18, **21**, **24**

E–109 4, 9, _____, _____, 24, 29, _____

E–110 25, 23, _____, _____, _____, 15, 13

E–111 _____, _____, 45, 50, 55, _____, _____

E–112 _____, 4, _____, _____, 10, 12, 14

E–113 4, 7, _____, _____, _____, 19, 22

E–114 _____, _____, 32, 29, 26, _____, _____

E–115 _____, 12, _____, 18, _____, 24, _____

© 1988 MIDWEST PUBLICATIONS   P.O. BOX 448, PACIFIC GROVE, CA 93950

SEQUENCES OF NUMBERS

The three dots mean that the sequence continues.
Remember that three dots do not stand for one dot per number.
Circle the row that belongs to the sequence.

Example:

3, 6, 9, 12 • • •

a.   18, 20, 22, 24

b.   25, 28, 31, 34

c.   30, 33, 36, 39

E–116

15, 20, 25, 30 • • •

a.   55, 60, 65, 70

b.   80, 75, 70, 65

c.   40, 50, 60, 70

E–117

5, 7, 9, 11 • • •

a.   22, 24, 26, 28

b.   13, 17, 21, 25

c.   19, 21, 23, 25

E–118

10, 12, 14, 16 • • •

a.   28, 26, 24, 22

b.   18, 22, 26, 30

c.   30, 32, 34, 36

E–119

4, 9, 14, 19 • • •

a.   34, 39, 44, 49

b.   24, 28, 32, 36

c.   37, 42, 47, 52

NUMBER MACHINES

The numbers in the boxes are put into number machines.
The numbers coming out are circled.
Find out what the machine in each exercise does to the numbers.
Fill in the blank circle.

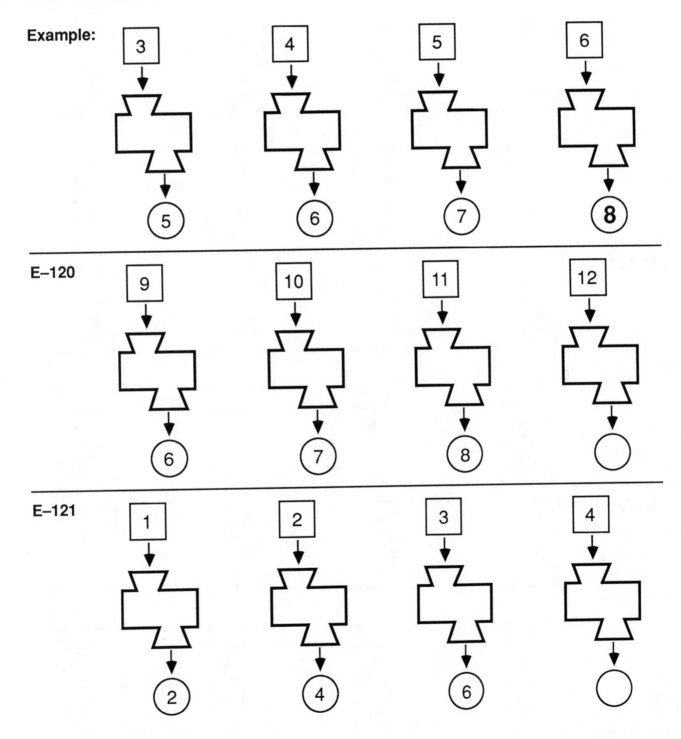

Example:

E–120

E–121

NUMBER MACHINES

The numbers in the boxes are put into number machines.
The numbers coming out are circled.
Find out what the machine in each exercise does to the numbers.
Fill in the blank circle.

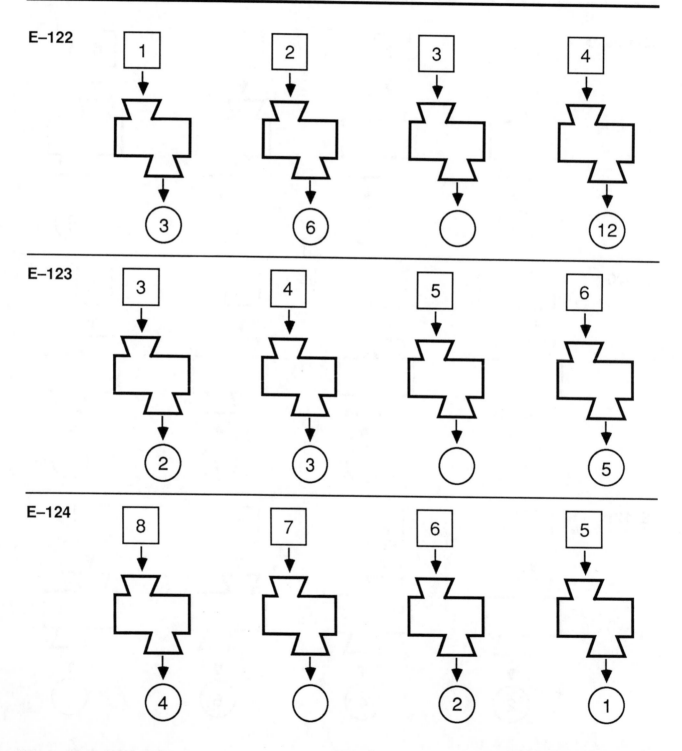

NUMBER MACHINES

The numbers in the boxes are put into number machines.
The numbers coming out are circled.
One of the circled numbers in each exercise is NOT correct.
Put an ✗ on the wrong answer.

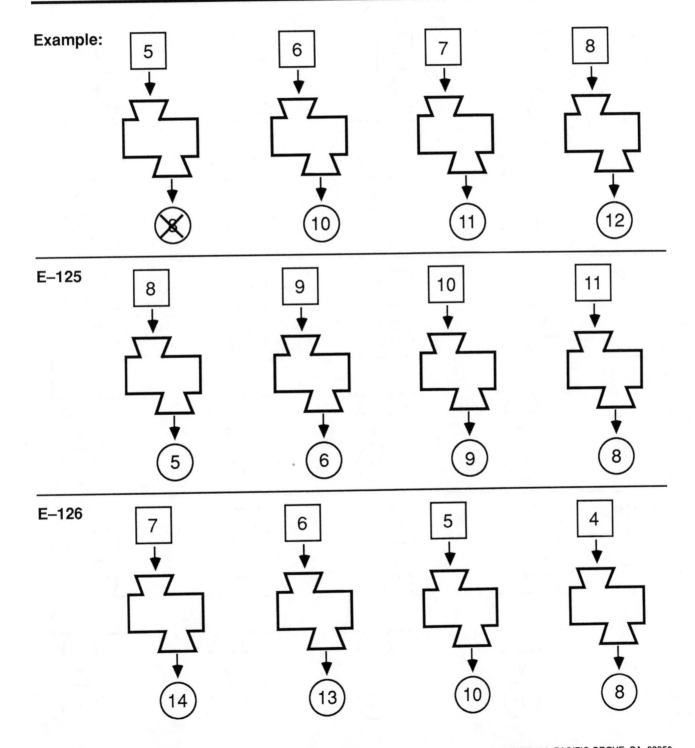

P.O. BOX 448, PACIFIC GROVE, CA 93950

NUMBER MACHINES

The numbers in the boxes are put into number machines.
The numbers coming out are circled.
One of the circled numbers in each exercise is NOT correct.
Put an ✕ on the wrong answer.

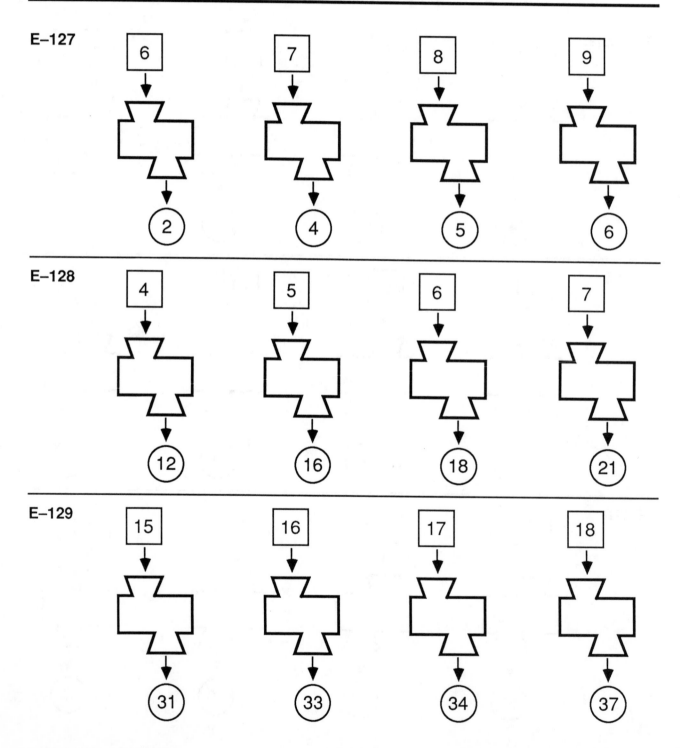

E–127

| 6 | 7 | 8 | 9 |

(2) (4) (5) (6)

E–128

| 4 | 5 | 6 | 7 |

(12) (16) (18) (21)

E–129

| 15 | 16 | 17 | 18 |

(31) (33) (34) (37)

NUMBER MACHINES

The numbers in the boxes are put into number machines. The numbers coming out are circled.
Find out what the machine in each exercise does to the numbers.
Note the three dots before the last machine.
Fill in the blank circle.

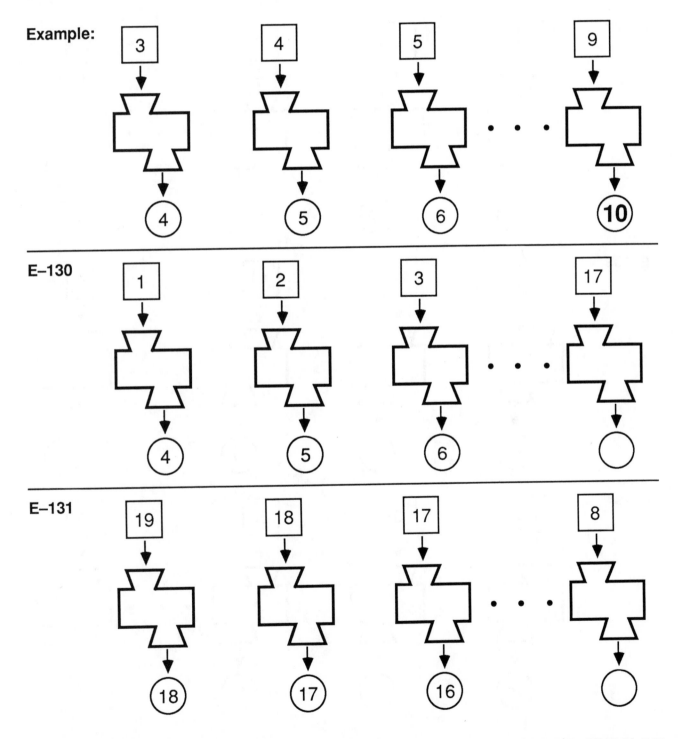

Example:

3 → 4
4 → 5
5 → 6 · · · · 9 → (10)

E–130

1 → 4
2 → 5
3 → 6 · · · · 17 → ( )

E–131

19 → 18
18 → 17
17 → 16 · · · · 8 → ( )

P.O. BOX 448, PACIFIC GROVE, CA 93950

NUMBER MACHINES

The numbers in the boxes are put into number machines. The numbers coming out are circled.
Find out what the machine in each exercise does to the numbers.
Note the three dots before the last machine.
Fill in the blank circle.

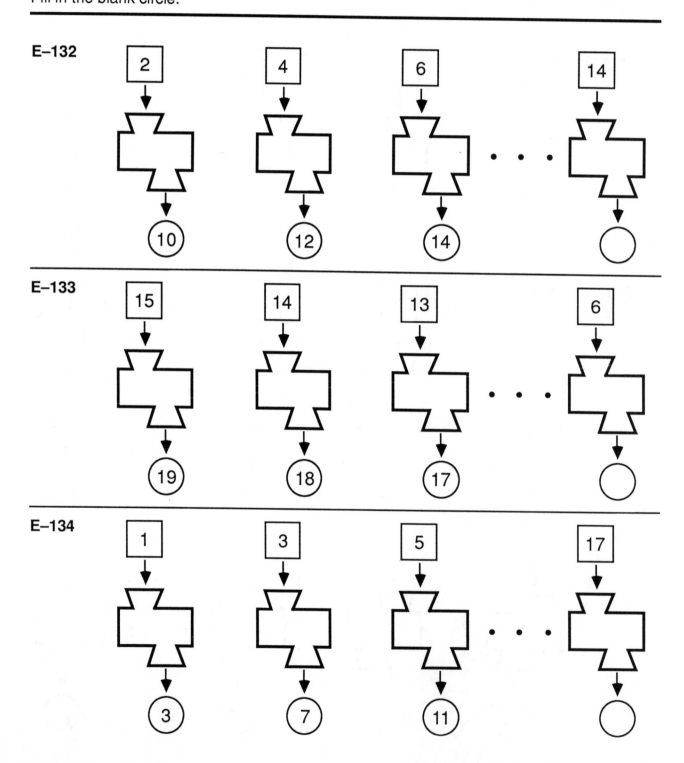

E–132

E–133

E–134

PAIRING NUMBERS

The arrows show that the numbers are paired.
Find out how the numbers are paired.
Fill in the circles with the missing numbers.

Example:

5	9	12	6	8	15	10
↓	↓	↓	↓	↓	↓	↓
4	8	11	5	(7)	(14)	(9)

E–135

2	5	3	1	7	9	10
↓	↓	↓	↓	↓	↓	↓
4	10	6	2	◯	◯	◯

E–136

3	2	9	6	12	5	7
↓	↓	↓	↓	↓	↓	↓
5	5	5	5	◯	◯	◯

E–137

7	3	10	5	1	12	8
↓	↓	↓	↓	↓	↓	↓
12	8	15	10	◯	◯	◯

E–138

11	4	9	7	14	6	3
↓	↓	↓	↓	↓	↓	↓
8	1	6	4	◯	◯	◯

247   P.O. BOX 448, PACIFIC GROVE, CA 93950

PAIRING NUMBERS

The arrows show that the numbers are paired.
Find out how the numbers are paired.
Fill in the circles with the missing numbers.

E–139

5	2	8	10	6	4	9
↓	↓	↓	↓	↓	↓	↓
15	6	24	30	◯	◯	◯

E–140

2	3	8	5	6	9	10
↓	↓	↓	↓	↓	↓	↓
0	1	0	1	◯	◯	◯

E–141

9	3	7	5	2	12	8
↓	↓	↓	↓	↓	↓	↓
19	13	17	15	◯	◯	◯

E–142

1	6	10	4	11	8	3
↓	↓	↓	↓	↓	↓	↓
2	2	2	2	◯	◯	◯

E–143

13	7	2	10	5	9	4
↓	↓	↓	↓	↓	↓	↓
11	5	0	8	◯	◯	◯

MULTIPLES OF 2, 3, AND 5

Draw a circle around all the multiples of 2.
Draw a square around all the multiples of 3.
Draw a triangle around all the multiples of 5.
Some numbers will have more than one shape around them.

Example:

1	②	[3]	4	△5
6	7	8	9	10
11	12	13	14	15
16	17	18	19	20
21	22	23	24	25
26	27	28	29	30

E–144   Which multiples of 2 are also multiples of 3?_____

E–145   Which multiples of 2 are also multiples of 5?_____

E–146   Which multiples of 3 are also multiples of 5?_____

E–147   Which numbers are multiples of all three numbers?_____

MULTIPLES OF 2, 3, AND 5

Example:

Circle all the
multiples of 2.

(12)	17	19	(18)
(24)	(8)	9	3
(10)	7	(40)	11

E–148

Circle all the
multiples of 3.

9	8	4	7
11	3	12	6
15	10	5	18

E–149

Circle all the
multiples of 5.

12	15	8	6
10	22	50	9
35	18	19	52

E–150

Circle all the
multiples of 2.

35	22	7	10
8	11	12	2
6	18	13	9

                                       P.O. BOX 448, PACIFIC GROVE, CA 93950

DIVISIBILITY

Example: Circle all the numbers divisible by 3.

  8   11

E–151   Circle all the numbers divisible by 2.

10   5   6   9   20

E–152   Circle all the numbers divisible by 5.

14   6   15   8   10

E–153   Circle all the numbers divisible by 3.

6   10   14   3   15

E–154   Circle all the numbers divisible by 2.

30   25   5   12   10

E–155   Circle all the numbers divisible by 5.

30   25   5   12   10

---

251   P.O. BOX 448, PACIFIC GROVE, CA 93950

DIVISIBILITY

Example: Divide each number by 2.
Circle all the numbers that leave a remainder of 1.

8		10		6

E–156   Divide each number by 3.
Circle all the numbers that leave a remainder of 1.

12	11	8	7	10

E–157   Divide each number by 3.
Circle all the numbers that leave a remainder of 2.

12	11	8	7	10

E–158   Divide each number by 2.
Circle all the numbers that leave a remainder of 1.

11	4	9	12	3

E–159   Divide each number by 5.
Circle all the numbers that leave a remainder of 1.

6	17	7	11	23

E–160   Divide each number by 5.
Circle all the numbers that leave a remainder of 2.

6	17	8	11	23

---

252   P.O. BOX 448, PACIFIC GROVE, CA 93950

SUMS WITH 1, 2, AND 3

Nine different addition exercises can be made using the numbers 1, 2, and 3.
Write 1, 2, or 3 in the boxes to make the nine different exercises.
Write their sums in the circles.

Example:

$$\boxed{2} + \boxed{3} = \bigcirc{5}$$

E–161

$$\square + \square = \bigcirc$$

E–162

$$\square + \square = \bigcirc$$

E–163

$$\square + \square = \bigcirc$$

E–164

$$\square + \square = \bigcirc$$

E–165

$$\square + \square = \bigcirc$$

E–166

$$\square + \square = \bigcirc$$

E–167

$$\square + \square = \bigcirc$$

E–168

$$\square + \square = \bigcirc$$

© 1988 MIDWEST PUBLICATIONS

P.O. BOX 448, PACIFIC GROVE, CA 93950

PRODUCTS WITH 2, 3, AND 5

Nine different multiplication exercises can be made using the numbers 2, 3, and 5.
Write 2, 3, or 5 in the boxes to make the nine different exercises.
Write their products in the circles.

Example:

$$\boxed{5} \times \boxed{3} = \bigcirc\!\!\!\!\!\!15$$

E–169

$$\boxed{} \times \boxed{} = \bigcirc$$

E–170

E–171

$$\boxed{} \times \boxed{} = \bigcirc$$

E–172

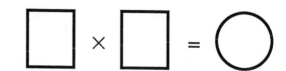

E–173

$$\boxed{} \times \boxed{} = \bigcirc$$

E–174

$$\boxed{} \times \boxed{} = \bigcirc$$

E–175

$$\boxed{} \times \boxed{} = \bigcirc$$

E–176

$$\boxed{} \times \boxed{} = \bigcirc$$

READING TABLES

The table shows the total number of students absent from school during one week.

Day	Number Absent
Monday	35
Tuesday	24
Wednesday	17
Thursday	19
Friday	30

Use the table to answer the following questions.

Example: On what day were most students absent?_____**Monday**_____

F–1　　How many students were absent on Friday?_____

F–2　　On what day were 24 students absent?_____

F–3　　On what day were the least number absent?_____

F–4　　What was the total number of students absent
　　　　during the week? _____

F–5　　Were there more students absent on Monday
　　　　or on Friday?_____

F–6　　Were there fewer students absent on Wednesday
　　　　or on Thursday?_____

READING TABLES

The table shows the number of miles between streets and certain places in Old Town.

MILES FROM STREETS TO PLACES

	Taylor School	Hope Theater	City Park	Town Hall
Hope Street	2	0	1	1
Main Street	1	1	2	0
Park Street	1	1	0	2
North Road	4	4	3	5
Elm Street	2	2	1	3

Use the table to answer the following questions.

Example: How many miles is it from Park Street to Town Hall?_____**2**_____

F–7   How many miles is it from Hope Street to City Park?_____

F–8   How many miles is it from North Road to the Hope Theater?_____

F–9   How many miles is Taylor School from Elm Street? _____

F–10   How many miles is City Park from Main Street?_____

F–11   On what street is Town Hall? _____

F–12   On what street is City Park?_____

F–13   Is Main Street or Hope Street further from City Park?_____

F–14   Is Town Hall or Taylor School further from Park Street?_____

COMPLETING A TABLE

An election was held to elect a student leader.
John got 6 votes, Amy got 8 votes, Karen got 4 votes, and Elaine got 11 votes.

Complete the table using the information given above.

	Name of Student	Number of Votes
Example:	Amy	**8**
F–15	Elaine	
F–16	John	
F–17	Karen	

Use the table to answer the following questions.

F–18   How many votes did Karen get? _____

F–19   Who got the least number of votes? _____

F–20   What was the total number of votes? _____

F–21   How many more votes did Amy get than Karen? _____

F–22   How many more votes did Elaine get than John? _____

F–23   Who won the election? _____

COMPLETING A TABLE

The number of students in Mr. Dodd's class that bought lunch on Monday was 20, on Tuesday 23, on Wednesday 19, on Thursday 24, and on Friday 21.
In Ms. Gilman's class there were 16 on Monday, 19 on Tuesday, 20 on Wednesday, 21 on Thursday, and 17 on Friday.

Complete the table using the information given above.

	Day	Mr. Dodd's Class	Ms. Gilman's Class
Example:	Monday	**20**	**16**
F–24	Tuesday		
F–25	Wednesday		
F–26	Thursday		
F–27	Friday		

Use the table to answer the following questions.

F–28   How many students in both classes bought lunch
on Wednesday?_____

F–29   How many students in both classes bought lunch on Friday?_____

F–30   What was the total number of lunches for the week in
Ms. Gilman's class?_____

F–31   On what day did the largest number of students
buy lunch?_____

F–32   On what day did the students buy the least number
of lunches?_____

CONSTRUCTING A TABLE

Amy, Elaine, and John used a map to find distances from their homes to places in town.
From Amy's home it is 1 mile to school, 2 miles to the park, and 3 miles to the theater.
From Elaine's home it is 1 mile to the park, 4 miles to school, and 3 miles to the theater.
From John's home it is 1 mile to school, 1 mile to the theater, and 5 miles to the park.

Complete the table using the information given above.

	DISTANCE TO		
	Park	Theater	School
F–33 Amy			
F–34 Elaine			
F–35 John			

Use the table to answer the following questions.

F–36   Who lives furthest from the school?_____

F–37   Who lives closest to the school?_____

F–38   How far is Elaine's home from the theater?_____

F–39   How far is the theater from John's home?_____

F–40   Who lives further from the park, Amy or Elaine?_____

F–41   Who lives closer to the theater, John or Elaine?_____

       P.O. BOX 448, PACIFIC GROVE, CA 93950

CONSTRUCTING A TABLE

In Mr. Dodd's class 8 students walk to school, 16 come by bus, and 5 come by car.
In Ms. Gilman's class 6 students walk, 8 come by car, and 14 by bus.

Complete the table using the information given above.

HOW STUDENTS COME TO SCHOOL

		Mr. Dodd's Class	Ms. Gilman's Class
F–42	Bus		
F–43	Car		
F–44	Walk		

Use the table to answer the following questions.

F–45   How many students in both classes take the bus?_____

F–46   Do more students in Mr. Dodd's class or Ms. Gilman's
class walk to school?_____

F–47   How many students are in Ms. Gilman's class?_____

F–48   How many students are in Mr. Dodd's class?_____

F–49   How many students in both classes ride to school?_____

F–50   Do more students in Mr. Dodd's class or Ms. Gilman's
class ride to school?_____

READING GRAPHS

The graph shows the high temperatures for each day during one week.

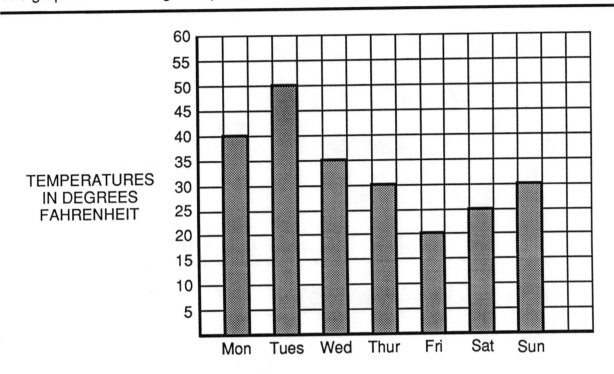

TEMPERATURES
IN DEGREES
FAHRENHEIT

Use the graph to answer the following questions.

Example: What was the high temperature on Saturday? _____**25°F**_____

F–51   What was the highest temperature during the week?_____

F–52   On what day was the high temperature 35° F?_____

F–53   On what day was the high temperature 20° F?_____

F–54   Was it warmer at the beginning or the end of the week?_____

F–55   Which two days had the same high temperature?_____

_____

READING GRAPHS

The graph shows the number of hours of sleep for a group of children.

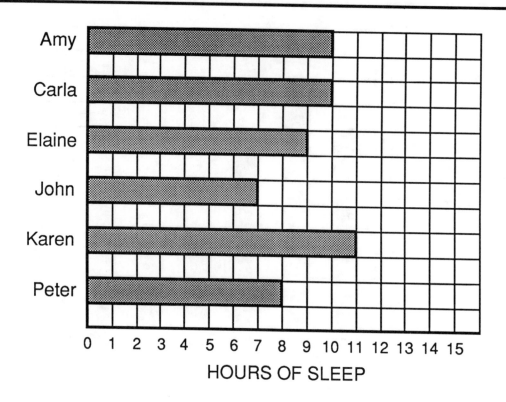

HOURS OF SLEEP

Use the graph to answer the following questions.

Example: How long did Elaine sleep?_____ **9 hours** _____

F–56   Who slept the largest number of hours?_____

F–57   Who slept the least number of hours?_____

F–58   Who slept 9 hours? _____

F–59   Which two people slept the same number of hours?_____

F–60   How many more hours did Karen sleep than John?_____

                                       P.O. BOX 448, PACIFIC GROVE, CA 93950

COMPLETING A GRAPH

The height of a plant was measured each week and was written in the table below.

Date	Height in Cm
June 1	2
June 8	2
June 15	4
June 22	6
June 29	10
July 6	16
July 13	18

Use the table to complete the following graph.

F–61

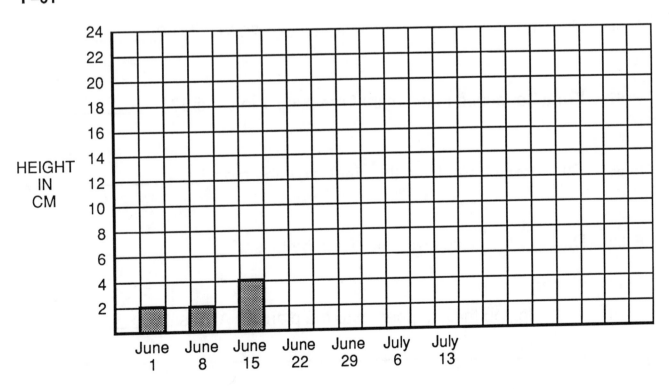

COMPLETING A GRAPH

The height of the plant in the last activity was measured three more times.
Enter the following measures on the graph of that activity on the preceding page.
The height was 20 cm on July 20, 20 cm on July 27, and 4 cm on August 5.

Use the graph on the preceding page to answer the following questions.

F–62　　What was the height of the plant on June 29?_____

F–63　　When did the plant measure 18 cm?_____

F–64　　What was the height of the plant on July 6?_____

F–65　　How much did the plant grow from June 15 to June 29?_____

F–66　　How much did the plant grow from June 29 to July 6?_____

F–67　　What happened to the plant from June 1 to June 8?_____

F–68　　During which week did the plant grow the most?_____

F–69　　During which week was the plant the tallest?_____

F–70　　What do you think happened to the plant on August 5?_____

_____

COMPLETING A GRAPH

In a class election each vote was marked with a √.
Here are the results.

Ann   √ √ √ √ √ √ √ √

Carla   √ √ √ √ √

Edward   √ √ √ √ √ √ √ √ √

Brian   √ √ √ √ √ √

Doug   √ √ √ √

Use the results to complete the following bar graph.

F–71

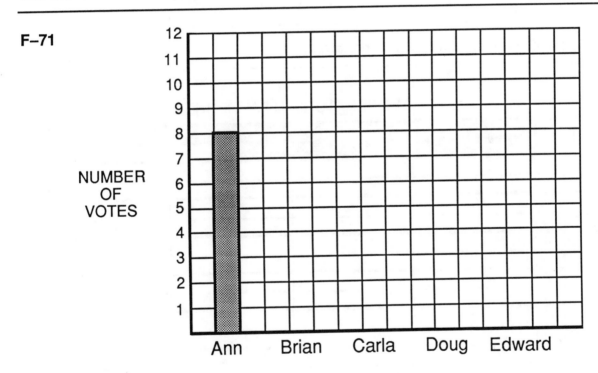

NUMBER OF VOTES

F–72   How many votes did Brian get?_____

F–73   Who won the election?_____

F–74   What was the total number of votes?_____

P.O. BOX 448, PACIFIC GROVE, CA 93950

COMPLETING A GRAPH

The high and low temperatures were recorded for each day of the week.

Day	TEMPERATURE IN FAHRENHEIT	
	High	Low
Monday	72	52
Tuesday	68	48
Wednesday	70	50
Thursday	74	52
Friday	76	56
Saturday	78	60
Sunday	80	68

Use the table to complete the following bar graph.

F–75

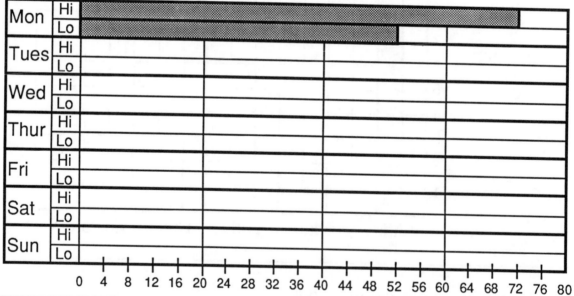

F–76 What was the highest temperature for the week?_____

F–77 What was the lowest temperature for the week?_____

P.O. BOX 448, PACIFIC GROVE, CA 93950

READING CHARTS

Each row in the seating plan is named with a letter.
Each chair is named with a number.

	A	B	C	D	E	F
4		Pat	Sara	Gerry		
3	Marie	Juanita	David		Elise	Debbie
2	Carlos		Chris	Harry	Cindy	Hector
1	Andy	Ann	Richard	Linda	Carol	

Circle the location of each person listed below.

Example:		**F–78**	
	a. **C4**	Elise	a. F2
Sara	b. B3		b. E3
	c. A1		c. D3
F–79		**F–80**	
	a. D1	Juanita	a. B3
Linda	b. D2		b. C4
	c. D3		c. D3
F–81		**F–82**	
	a. A2	Hector	a. A4
Chris	b. B2		b. C2
	c. C2		c. F2

LOCATING POSITIONS IN A CHART

Each row in the seating plan is named with a letter.
Each chair is named with a number.

	A	B	C	D	E	F
4		Pat	Sara	Gerry		
3	Marie	Juanita	David		Elise	Debbie
2	Carlos		Chris	Harry	Cindy	Hector
1	Andy	Ann	Richard	Linda	Carol	

Write the location of each person listed below.

Example: Elise _____**E3**_____   **F–83** Debbie _____

F–84 Chris _____   **F–85** Marie _____

F–86 Gerry _____   **F–87** Ann _____

F–88 Write the locations of the empty seats in the chart. _____

F–89 Write the location of the person between Harry and Hector. _____

F–90 Write the location of the person between Richard and Andy. _____

F–91 Write the locations of the people in front of Marie. _____

READING CHARTS

Each row in the seating plan is named with a letter.
Each chair is named with a number.

	A	B	C	D	E	F
4		Pat	Sara	Gerry		
3	Marie	Juanita	David ✓		Elise	Debbie
2	Carlos		(Chris)	Harry	Cindy	Hector
1	Andy	Ann	Richard ✗	Linda	Carol	

Circle the names of the people seated in the locations in the box.

F–92

C2, E2, D2, F2

Put an ✗ on the names of the people seated in the locations in the box.

F–93

C1, C3, C4, C2

Put a ✓ on the names of the people seated in the locations in the box.

F–94

C3, E1, B4, D2

Circle the locations in the list below that are empty seats.

F–95

B2, C2, D3, A2, E3, A4, F1, F2

P.O. BOX 448, PACIFIC GROVE, CA 93950

READING CHARTS

Each row in the seating plan is named with a letter.
Each chair is named with a number.

	A	B	C	D	E	F
4		Pat	Sara	Gerry		
3	Marie	Juanita	David		Elise	Debbie
2	Carlos		Chris	Harry	Cindy	Hector
1	Andy	Ann	Richard	Linda	Carol	

Write the name of each person in the seats listed below.

Example: seat D4   **Gerry**   **F–96**   seat C3 _____

F–97   seat B4 _____   **F–98**   seat F2 _____

F–99   seat A2 _____   **F–100**   seat B1 _____

F–101 Write the name of the person seated between C2 and E2. _____

F–102 Write the name of the person seated between C3 and A3. _____

F–103 Write the names of the people seated behind E1. _____

F–104 Write the names of the people seated in front of B4. _____

 P.O. BOX 448, PACIFIC GROVE, CA 93950

LOCATING POSITIONS ON A CHART

Each column in the chart is named with a letter.
Each row in the chart is named with a number.

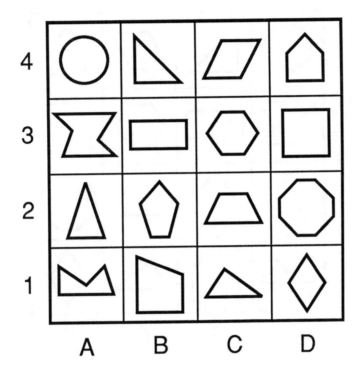

Write the locations of the figures given in the exercises below.

Example: _____ **A 4**

F–105 _____

F–106 _____

F–107 _____

F–108 _____

F–109 _____

F–110 _____

F–111 _____

271   P.O. BOX 448, PACIFIC GROVE, CA 93950

READING CHARTS

Each column in the chart is named with a letter.
Each row in the chart is named with a number.

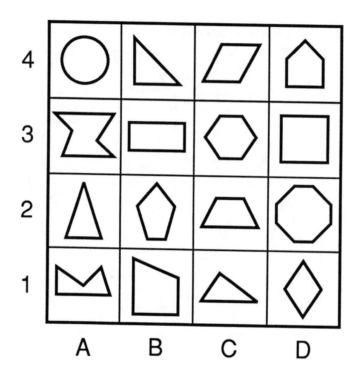

Draw the figures from the chart above next to their locations given below.

Example: B 3 _____

F–113   A 2 _____

F–115   A 4 _____

F–117   D 4 _____

F–112   D 3 _____

F–114   C 2 _____

F–116   C 4 _____

F–118   B 1 _____

READING CHARTS

Each column in the chart is named with a letter.
Each row in the chart is named with a number.

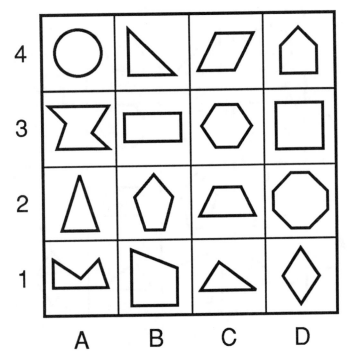

Find the figures listed in the boxes below.
Match the groups of figures with their properties.

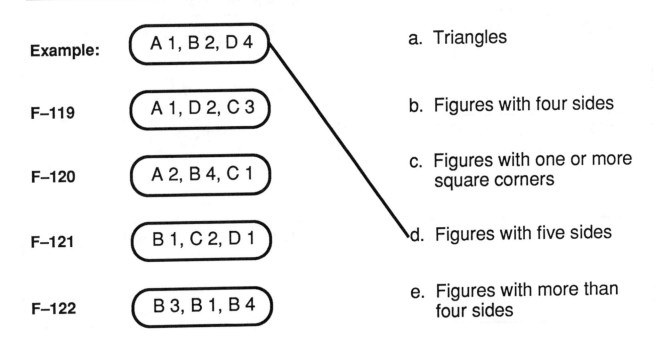

Example: A 1, B 2, D 4

a. Triangles

F–119 A 1, D 2, C 3

b. Figures with four sides

F–120 A 2, B 4, C 1

c. Figures with one or more square corners

F–121 B 1, C 2, D 1

d. Figures with five sides

F–122 B 3, B 1, B 4

e. Figures with more than four sides

P.O. BOX 448, PACIFIC GROVE, CA 93950

READING CHARTS

Each column in the chart is named with a letter.
Each row in the chart is named with a number.

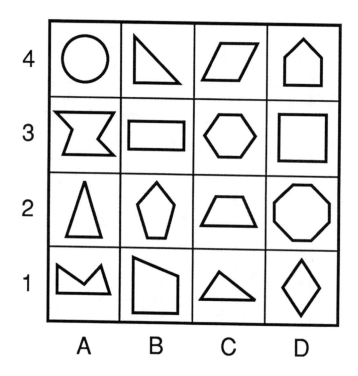

Draw the figures below that are in the following locations on the chart.

Example:	Between B 3 and D 3	**F–123**	Between C 2 and A 2
F–124	Between D 2 and D 4	**F–125**	Between A 3 and A 1
F–126	Below B 2	**F–127**	Above B 2

P.O. BOX 448, PACIFIC GROVE, CA 93950

LOCATING POINTS ON A GRAPH

Each vertical line of the graph is named with a letter.
Each horizontal line of the graph is named with a number.
Put an ✗ on the graph for each point listed in the box.

Example:

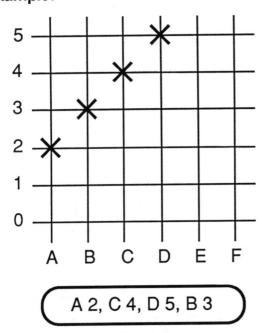

A 2, C 4, D 5, B 3

F–128

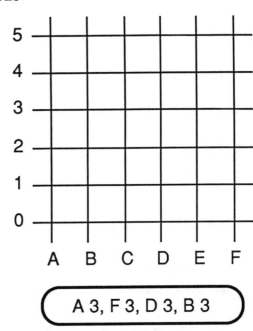

A 3, F 3, D 3, B 3

F–129

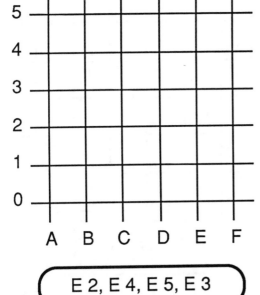

E 2, E 4, E 5, E 3

F–130

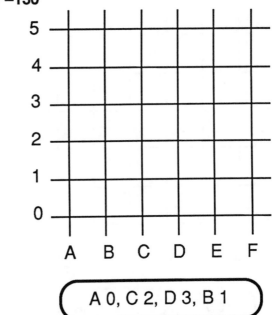

A 0, C 2, D 3, B 1

P.O. BOX 448, PACIFIC GROVE, CA 93950

LOCATING POINTS ON A GRAPH

Each vertical line of the graph is named with a letter.
Each horizontal line of the graph is named with a number.
Put an on the graph for each point listed in the box.

F–131

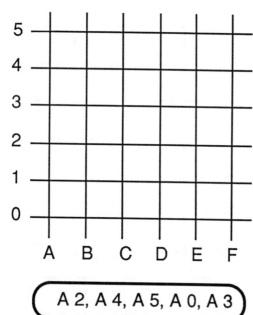

A 2, A 4, A 5, A 0, A 3

F–132

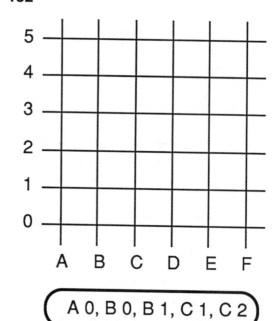

A 0, B 0, B 1, C 1, C 2

F–133

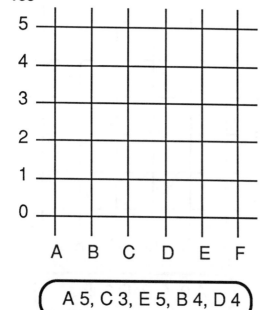

A 5, C 3, E 5, B 4, D 4

F–134

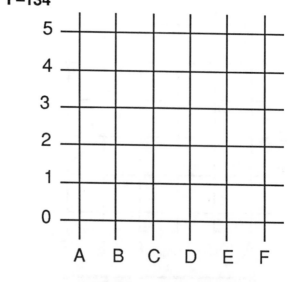

A 0, A 1, B 1, B 2, C 2

P.O. BOX 448, PACIFIC GROVE, CA 93950

READING GRAPHS

Each vertical line of the graph is named with a letter.
Each horizontal line of the graph is named with a number.
Write the location of each ✕ in the box.

Example:

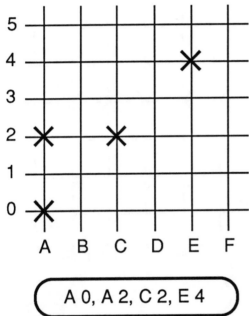

A 0, A 2, C 2, E 4

F–135

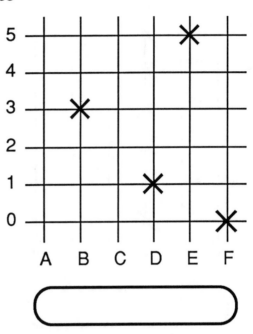

F–136

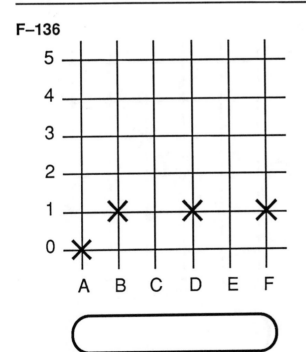

F–137

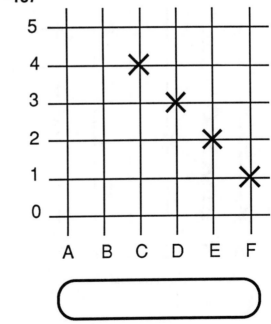

P.O. BOX 448, PACIFIC GROVE, CA 93950

READING GRAPHS

Each vertical line of the graph is named with a letter.
Each horizontal line of the graph is named with a number.
Write the location of each ✕ in the box.

F–138

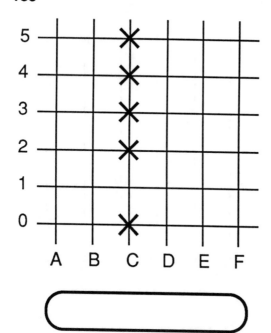

F–139

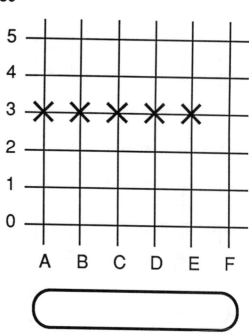

F–140

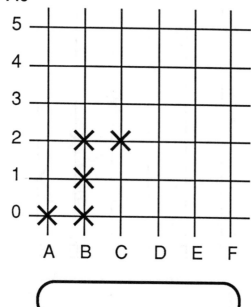

F–141

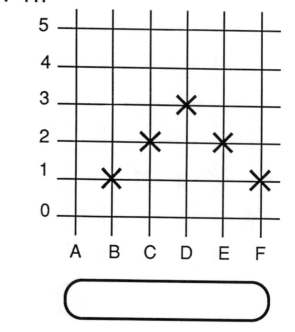

READING GRAPHS

Each vertical line of the graph is named with a letter.
Each horizontal line of the graph is named with a number.
Five points on the graph are connected with a line.
Write the locations of the points that the line connects.

Example:

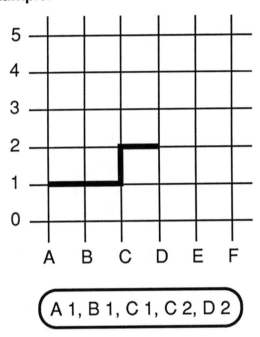

A 1, B 1, C 1, C 2, D 2

F–142

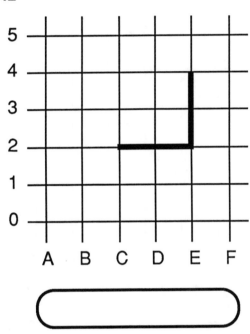

F–143

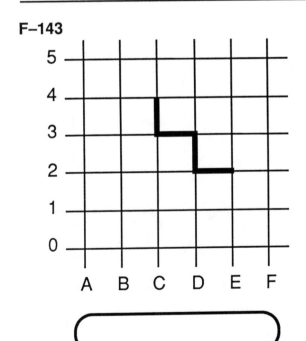

F–144

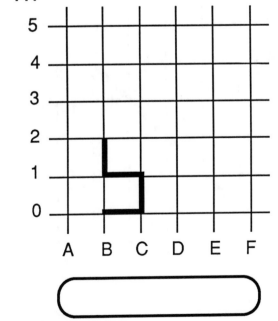

P.O. BOX 448, PACIFIC GROVE, CA 93950

READING GRAPHS

Each vertical line of the graph is named with a letter.
Each horizontal line of the graph is named with a number.
Five points on the graph are connected with a line.
Write the locations of the points that the line connects.

F–145

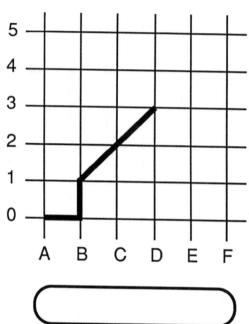

F–146

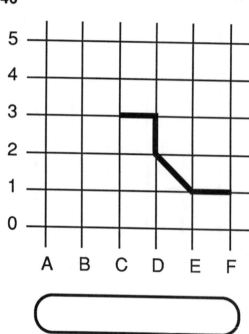

F–147

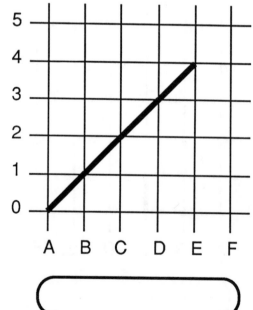

F–148

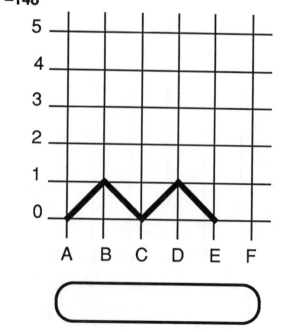

DRAWING GRAPHS

Each vertical line of the graph is named with a letter.
Each horizontal line of the graph is named with a number.
Draw a line to connect the points in the order that they are listed.

Example:

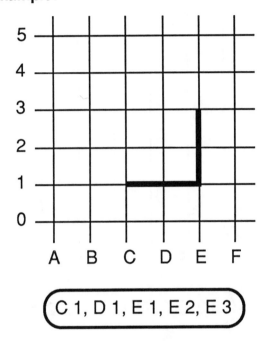

C 1, D 1, E 1, E 2, E 3

F–149

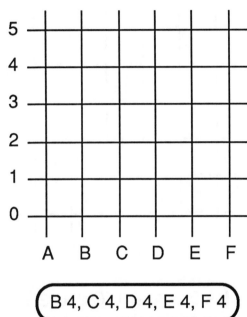

B 4, C 4, D 4, E 4, F 4

F–150

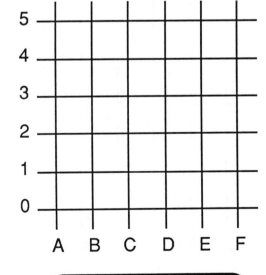

C 4, D 4, E 4, E 3, F 3

F–151

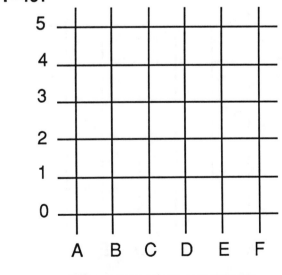

A 0, B 0, B 1, C 1, C 2

281   P.O. BOX 448, PACIFIC GROVE, CA 93950

DRAWING GRAPHS

Each vertical line of the graph is named with a letter.
Each horizontal line of the graph is named with a number.
Draw a line to connect the points in the order that they are listed.

F–152

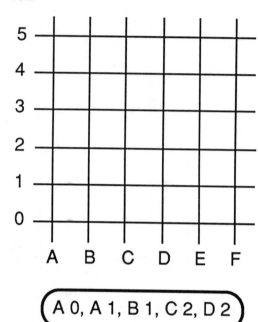

A 0, A 1, B 1, C 2, D 2

F–153

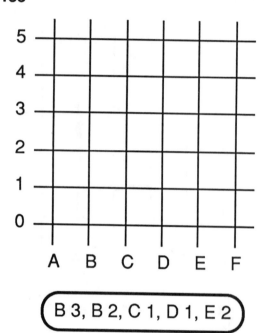

B 3, B 2, C 1, D 1, E 2

F–154

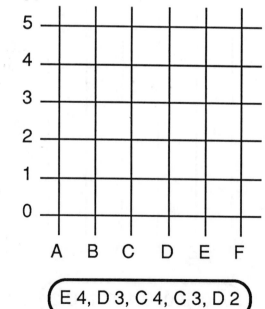

E 4, D 3, C 4, C 3, D 2

F–155

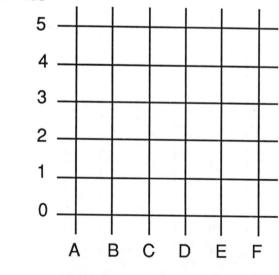

D 3, C 4, B 3, C 2, D 3

282   P.O. BOX 448, PACIFIC GROVE, CA 93950